NORTH BY NORTH

SCANDINAVIAN GRAPHIC DESIGN

Edited by Robert Klanten and Hendrik Hellige. Features by Goddur, Thomas Hilland and Kaliber10000. Interviews with Sweden and Ekhorn Forss/Non-Format.

NORTH BY NORTH

REMIX

The Earth Script As I cast an eye over the continents, mirroring my status as an islander, a graphic artist from that little rock of lava in the North Atlantic Ocean, I ask myself: How do my eyes select? What is the selective vision that determines this picture I see in the mirror here and now? Can a graphic artist represent his nation abroad in the same way as a chess player, a long distance runner or a musician – like Sigur Ros, Mum and Björk, of course? Is nationality the main concern for identity? Do we create islands that bear no relation to the rest of the world? That's not the picture I perceive.

Up here in Europe's most north-western corner creation has literally continued, from one millennium to the next, in a never-ending process: Volcanic eruptions, geysers and lava fields; earthquakes and ever-widening rifts in the island's interior, new mountains and new islands in recent decades; and, about six years ago, a volcanic eruption just below Europe's largest glacier, the first such creational event in the annals of modern science; which melted a 600-metre thick block of ice and demonstrated beyond doubt who is the Master of the Universe. Despite the combined strength of our scientific and technical knowledge we, the bearers of modern civilisation, have not yet reached such levels of power. In many ways the influence and inspiration of having grown up in such direct contact with the creative forces of nature has, in Iceland, bred a culture dominated by a considerable emphasis on the creative capabilities of every islander. To farmers as much as fishermen it is natural to be an innovator, to produce verse and short poems on the spur of the moment, to voice profound philosophical views on matters of state and global importance. No big deal! They don't buy art or design – they do it themselves! A great portion of literature was original however, composed by Icelanders and based in part on traditional tales about ancient times. The Eddic poems about heathen gods and Germanic heroes during the period of Germanic migrations were written down, while prose sagas were produced about events in Iceland and neighbouring countries dating from the earliest period of Icelandic settlement up unto the fourteenth century. This literature has been a constant element in the culture of Icelanders ever since it was first committed to vellum as an organic shape language using mother earth as its inspiration. Through the centuries, Icelandic literature has been copied and pasted time and again, more or less unchanged, inasmuch as the vocabulary of the ancient language has, for the most part, been preserved to this day, and changes in the grammar have been few. At the same time new Icelandic literature continued to be produced over the centuries, for profit and delight, in verse and prose; this was seldom printed, however, but is never-theless preserved in manuscripts, sometimes visually embellished in the spirit of our love of ancient ornamentation, a legacy from our Celtic connection which maybe explains why some design from the north is still closely connected with craft, and therefore a bridge to prevailing international ideas about the "role" of design which often tend to make everything look the same.

The Water Script The language of graphics. Intellectual cognition and the forming of logical conclusions – thinking that facilitates cognition and judgement. Why is it that Icelandic contemporary graphic design shows such strong symptoms of vernacular or homemade takes on modernism/post-modernism? Why are the ideas not original – just the solutions? The philosopher would say: Let a heavy stone fall into still waters, and surging waves will sweep in all directions... they are strongest near the centre and as they move outward they will start to break on small rocks in a changeable environment– but the change of shape will only be slight – their inherent nature will stay the same. For reasons not easily explained, but to a large degree due to economic and spiritual conditions, centres develop for new advances or the birth of new cultural ideas. Ideas that then spread throughout the world like the waves from a big stone that is thrown into the still waters of a quiet pond. Just think of Renaissance Florence or Venice, Paris in the first decades of this century or New York after the second world war.

Scandinavian design, a term coined in the 1950s, has been a powerful slogan – almost a burden too heavy to carry for its originators, stifling the spirit. But Scandinavian graphics has been a non-existent term. Perhaps the little that has been available got snowed under by the visual strength of other countries. These northern countries consider Iceland as one of their own. This is more than a current trend, it's a historical fact. But when it comes to compilation books they more often than not forget about us. The fact is that many groundbreaking artists come and fall in love with this country. They leave a driftwood of ideas – the turmoil and flux of the past. William Morris went up north, Dieter Roth went up north, Donald Judd went up north – and so do many contemporary artists on an international level, people like Roni Horn or Richard Long to name but a few. To know history is to know destiny. The less you know history - the more you are like everybody else. The history of movements, individuals and originals. It is the driftwood of time: traceable moments, picked out of the sea of history, pieces that have caught someone's attention because of their colour, or their shape, or because they were concepts that deviated from the norm, from what had come before, or because they had the power to drift further than the other pieces around it, or because others had called their attention to it. Reduce! – go to the line where you are ready to forget – You have to forget what you are to discover your individuality. "The key to creativity is bad memory!" – if I remember right – Miles Davis! – Be an individual to be an original!

The Air Script The Nordic Transparency - transparency in itself is a symbol of air. Air stands for emotions. Feeling is down to subjective evaluation – feeling should tell us how and to what extent a thing is important or unimportant to us. It is the choice of our surroundings. At least fifteen different names for snow. It is when landscape begins to shape our imagination, desires and dreams. Has your gaze been falling northwards? Have you, too, been looking north? It is in the magic moments, moods of nature, the sparkle of light, the mists of melancholy and the world of inaccessible images inside the ice mass. Winter wonderland itself - in transparent layers upon layers, in the work of a young graphic artist. It is in the song of the whale. It is the summer solstice – the midnight summer dream. The song of free birds. It is the twilight zone. It is in the uplift from hot rocks and the

drag of air over cool damp seas, in the uneven turbulence inside clouds, the drafts of dry winds. It is in the snow blizzards – icy shores, frozen seas – where sunrise and dusk are seasonal rather than daily phenomena. It is where an aurora erupts into space - greyish-greenish "bars" make the long journey across the sky, slight undulations, and a touch of purple during its passage. Sometimes this happens just after midnight. As if someone lit those "bars", for suddenly they are all energy. Fold upon fold of these translucent purplish-green lights run up and down the arcs (which cover an area of the sky roughly equal to, say, the Milky Way). Transparency upon transparency over and over again (impossible to focus on any one of them) – and yet delicate, very delicate. Stars can easily be seen through the aurora's light. If there is any single prevailing idea in the cultures of these "high north" countries with the appealing name of ULTIMA THULE, it is the search for continuity and a way of emphasising primitive forces and weight.

The Fire Scipt Some of the ancient Nordic symbols have been considered untouchable because of their association with Nazism, but runes and ancient symbols are parts of our global heritage, not just in Iceland, and didn't acquire these negative connotations until WW2. The legacy of the Mayas, the Egyptians and many others have preserved some kind of mysticism, free of these associations. US film-makers have filled our cinemas with movies using these symbols as a part of the so-called Marshall Plan. Should we demonise the Christian Cross just because of the situation in Palestine? Of course not – or maybe we should! Today even the stiff, sterile, angular and geometric expressions of Modernism evoke fascist authoritarian connotations in our minds and are emotionally perceived as the essential device of global corporate ID – the ubiquitous use of typefaces such as Helvetica and Universe represents globalisation and an authority stronger than anything else in existence nowadays. Initially launched to free us from nationalism and to represent internationalism as a more noble goal, the quest for universal objective truth has been distorted. This calls for the use of dirt and fertile vernacular!

Ancient graphics are often archetypes of a religious nature which reflect visions of the world. They represent the hidden possibilities in the background of reality which cannot easily be communicated other than with symbols, similes or codes. They belong to the completeness of a given situation. From them you can verbally tell stories. From them you can explain the vision of the world as graphic similes. Like other religions, Nordic mythology has an explanation of how the world was created and how it will cease to exist. The story about the creation of the world goes something like this: In the beginning there was only an empty void, Ginnungagap, in the middle of the world between the icy Niflheimar in the north and the red hot Muspelheimar in the south. There were no men or animals, nor sky, sea or ground. But as the glaciers pushed forward into the empty gap they met the heat from Muspelheimar and drops of vapour became alive and formed the jötunn (giant) Ymir and the cow Audhumbla. Audhumbla licked on the great salt rock, and the rock became a big, strong and beautiful man called Búri. Búri had a son named Bur, and he in turn had three sons: Odin, Vil and Vé. They killed Ymir and brought him to the middle of the empty void and created the Earth from his body: the flesh became the ground, the blood the sea, the bones the mountains and the teeth became loose rocks. From the brain heavy clouds were formed. His skull was put up as the firmament and four dwarfs: Austri (the East), Vestri (the West), Sudri (the South) and Nordri (the North) were placed in each corner to carry it. Sparks still came out of Muspelheimar, they formed the stars and planets that wander across the sky. Also the Sun and the Moon were created in this way. They travelled so fast across the sky on their wagons because they were chased by a pack of hungry wolfs. Sometimes a wolf manages to catch the Moon and takes larger and larger bites out of it, until in the end it drowns in blood. Thus, the Vikings explained a lunar eclipse. These, too, are graphics - astral graphics!

Man lived in Midgardur, while the gods themselves lived in Asgardur highest up. Asgardur can only be reached by crossing over Bifrost. That is the Aurora Borealis, the moving waves man can see in the northern hemisphere, but nobody knows where they end. The red band seen in the northern lights is flames and therefore no jötunn dared to enter the home of the gods until Ragnarök, the end of the World. On a starry night we can experience many of the star patterns or star graphics our ancestors visualised a thousand years ago. The most well-known star pattern in Scandinavia is Karlsvagninn (the Big Dipper), which is really a part of the constellation Ursa Major (the Great Bear). The Vikings believed Karlsvagninn was the carriage of Thor, the Thunder God, who gave his name to the fourth day of the week, Thursday. When Thor rode his carriage across the sky, pulled by two goats, lightning flashed from the rims and thunder rumbled from the wheels. Thus, the Vikings could explain the phenomena of thunder and lightning. Thor's weapon was his hammer Mjölnir, which never missed its target and always returned to the hand of its owner.

But the greatest achievement is perhaps their voyages across the North Atlantic to discover this island, Iceland, Greenland and North America. Here landfall was no longer possible and old records indicate that the Vikings used latitudinal navigation from Norway to Greenland, keeping their ships on the same latitude as judged by the positions of celestial objects. In mid-summer, when the sea is calmest and most journeys were made, it is hard to follow north by north – to observe the North Star in the twilight that lasts all night. Instead, the Vikings might have used a solar compass. This consists of a small disc with a gnomon in the middle. On the disc a curve is drawn, marking the path, the shadow of the gnomon will follow the latitude in question for the days around the summer solstice. If the shadow becomes too long the ship has drifted to the north and visa versa and the course can be corrected accordingly. This is using imagination as a possibility of reality. Beauty is our closest contact to the future. He who has imagination without visual references has wings without feet. To put your life in the hands of a mightier power is the paradox of originality. Our ancestors knew this but we, the bearers of modern civilisation, are confused. Are we heading towards a new Middle Ages?

Cut-up text pasted by Gudmundur Oddur Magnusson - goddur - Director of studies in graphic design at Iceland Academy of the Arts

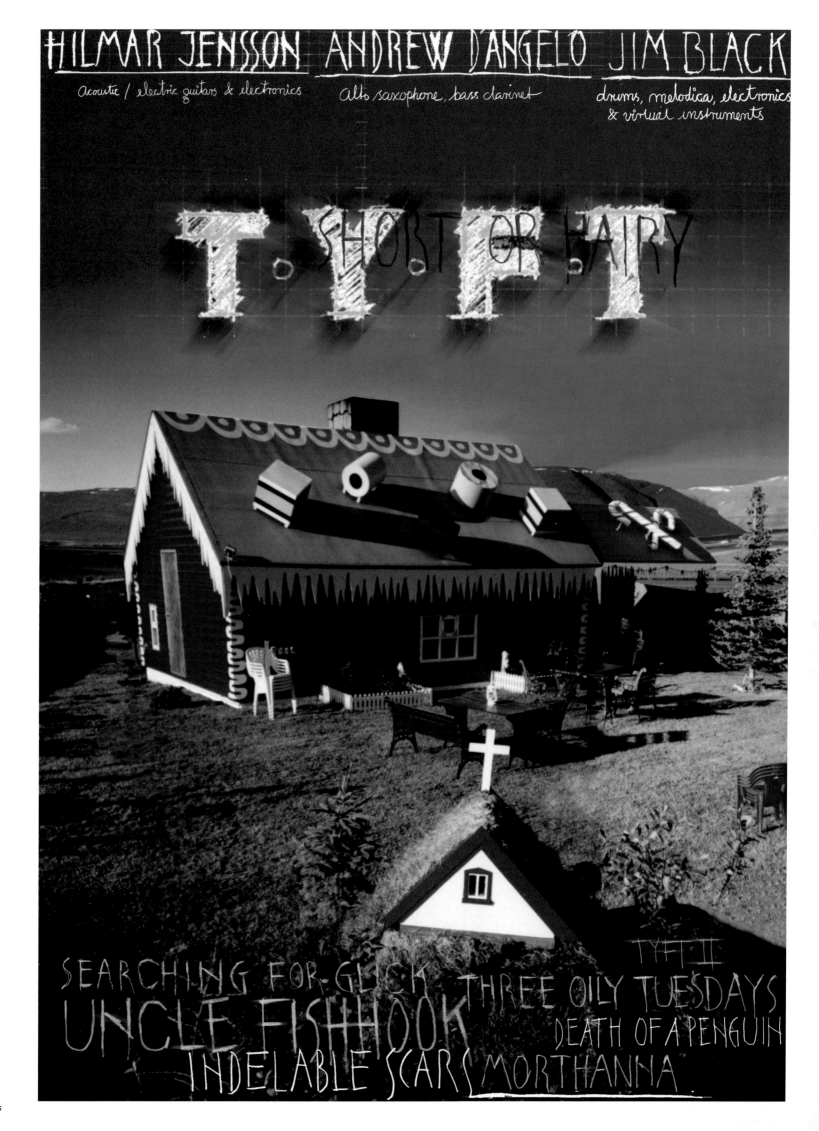

GODDUR Poster

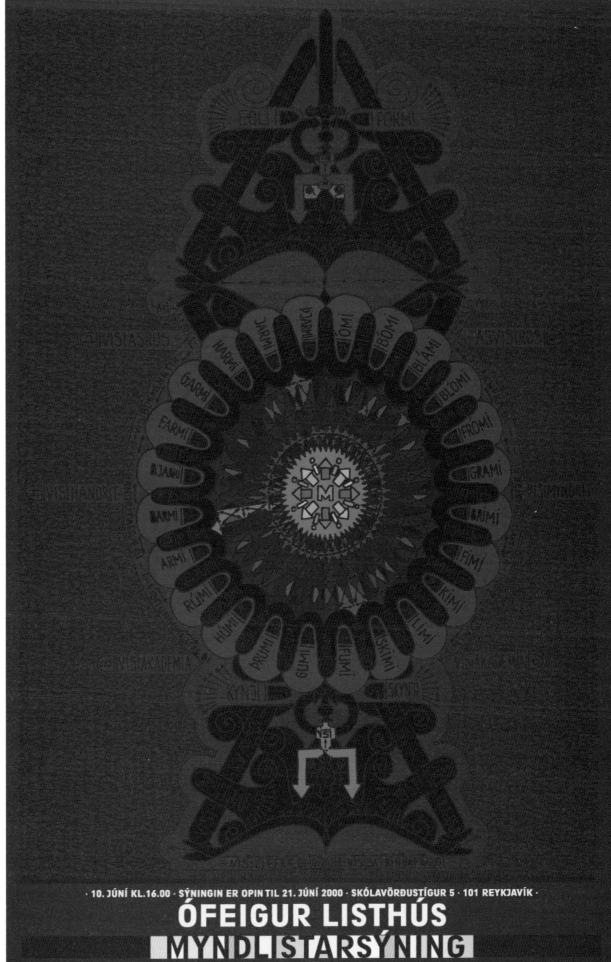

• 10. JÚNÍ KL.16.00 · SÝNINGIN ER OPIN TIL 21. JÚNÍ 2000 · SKÓLAVÖRÐUSTÍGUR 5 · 101 REYKJAVÍK ·

ÓFEIGUR LISTHÚS
MYNDLISTARSÝNING
· BJARNI H. ÞÓRARINSSON ·
SJÓNHÁTTARFRÆÐINGUR

GUÐMUNDUR ODDUR MAGNÚSSON
GRAFÍSKUR HÖNNUÐUR
· MÓTSTAÐUR 2 · SJÁVER · ÍSVÍS · VÍSIAKADEMÍA ·

GODDUR Poster

007

NORD JAZZ TOUR 98

ANN-SOFI SØDERQUIST & CHRISTINA NIELSEN QUINTET

30.11	Sundswal Jazzklubb (S)
01.12	Bolnäs (S)
02.12	Hernösand (S)
03.12	TBA
04.12	Jazzklubb Fasching Stockholm (S)
05.12	Gävle Koncerthus (S)
06.12	TBA
07.12	Jazz It-Oslo (N)
08.12	Stadthotellet-Hässelholm Jazzklubb (S)
09.12	Jazz i Helsingborg (S)
10.12	
11.12	Copenhagen Jazzhouse (DK)

SAMULI MIKKONEN TRIO feat. Anders Jormin og Audun Kleive

02.12	
03.12	Urijazz - Tønsberg (N)
04.12	Huset i Hasserisgade-Aalborg (DK)
05.12	Savoy Theatre-Helsinki (SF)
06.12	Recording
07.12	Recording

NIKLAS WINTHER JAZZWORKSHOP feat. Severi Pysalo

08.10	Musikcafeen - Århus (DK)
09.10	Carusel - Helsinki (SF)
10.10	TBA
11.10	Recording
12.10	Recording
13.10	TBA
14.10	TBA
15.10	TBA
16.10	TBA
17.10	Doo-Bop Club - Vaasa (SF)
18.10	TBA
19.10	TBA
20.10	Jazz Fyn (DK)

THE THULE SPIRIT PERFORMED BY NORTHERN VOICES

30.09	Copenhagen Jazzhouse (DK)
02.10	Bergen Jazzforum (N)
03.10	Nefertiti - Göteborg (S)
05.10	Savoy Theatre - Helsinki (SF)
06.10	Jazzclub Fasching - Stockholm (S)
07.10	Slagelse Musikhus (DK)
08.10	Magasinet - Odense (DK)
09.10	Musik teatret - Albertslund (DK)
10.10	Musikcaféen - Aarhus (DK)
11.10	Musikhuset Esbjerg (DK)

BLIXBAND

10.11	Bø Vertshus (N)
11.11	
12.11	Blå Jazzklubb (N)
13.11	TBA
14.11	Hotell Gyldenløve (N)
18.11	TBA
19.11	Christiansunds Jazzclub (N)
20.11	Bergen Jazzforum (N)
21.11	Kulturhuset Fraktgodsen (N)
22.11	
23.11	Tavastia Club - Helsinki (SF)
24.11	Jazzclub Fasching - Stockholm (S)
25.11	Copenhagen Jazzhouse (DK)
26.11	Musikcafeen - Aarhus (DK)
27.11	Nefertiti - Göteborg (S)

E-TYPES Poster

OSLO
INTERNATIONAL
FILM FESTIVAL

november 15–25

2001

oslofilmfestival.com

10 OSLO INTERNATIONAL FILMFESTIVAL

16.11.-26.11.2000

SUPERSTAR Poster

010

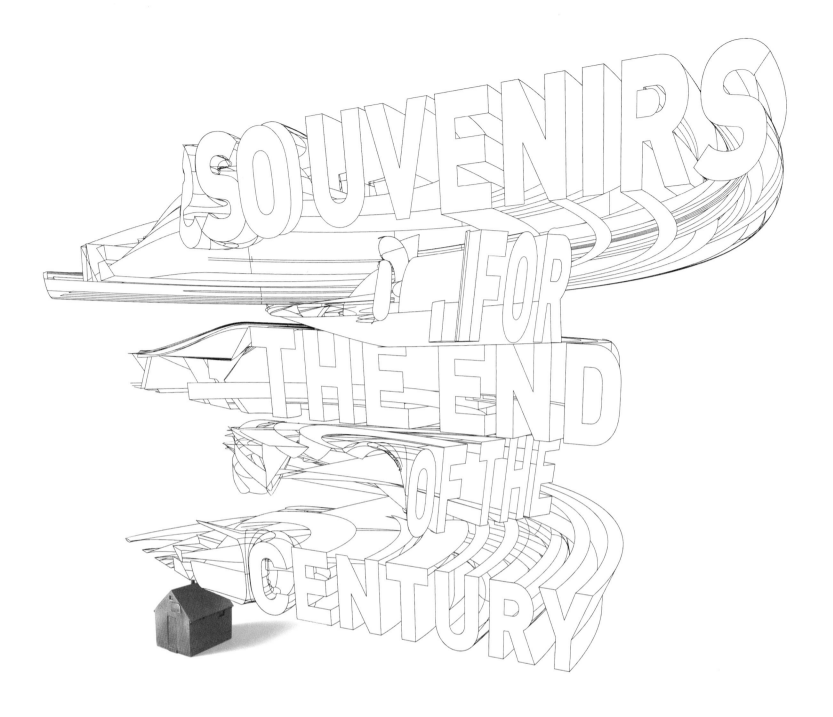

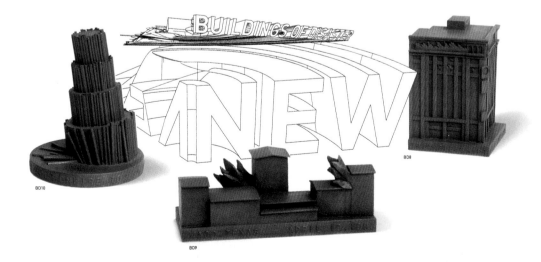

BD10

BD9

BD8

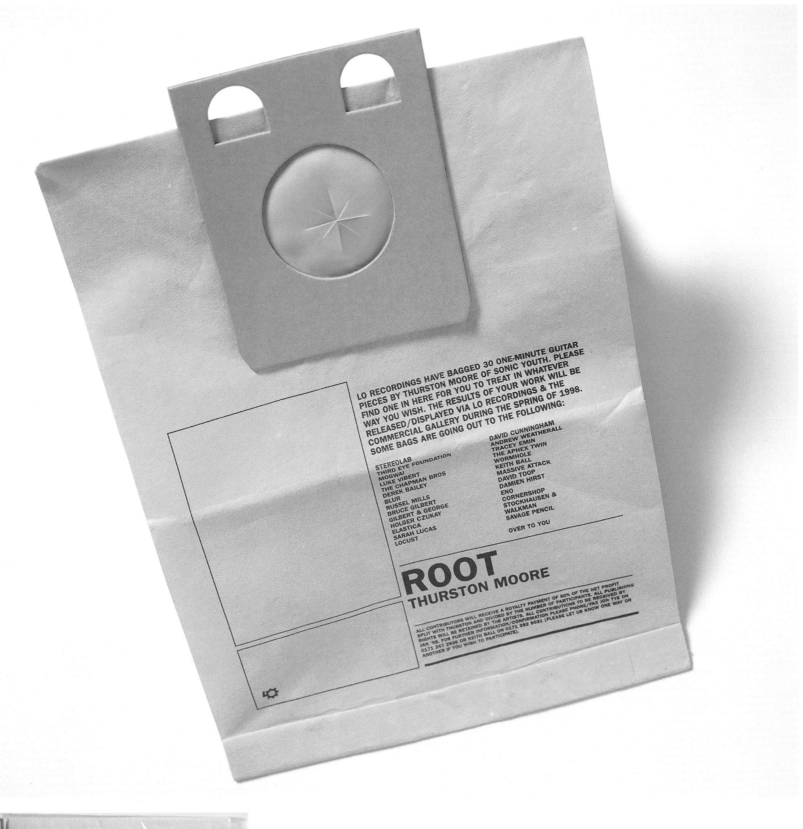

LO RECORDINGS HAVE BAGGED 30 ONE-MINUTE GUITAR
PIECES BY THURSTON MOORE OF SONIC YOUTH. PLEASE
FIND ONE IN HERE FOR YOU TO TREAT IN WHATEVER
WAY YOU WISH. THE RESULTS OF YOUR WORK WILL BE
RELEASED/DISPLAYED VIA LO RECORDINGS & THE
COMMERCIAL GALLERY DURING THE SPRING OF 1998.
SOME BAGS ARE GOING OUT TO THE FOLLOWING:

STEREOLAB
THIRD EYE FOUNDATION
MOGWAI
LUKE VIBERT
THE CHAPMAN BROS
DEREK BAILEY
BLUR
RUSSEL MILLS
BRUCE GILBERT
GILBERT & GEORGE
HOLGER CZUKAY
ELASTICA
SARAH LUCAS
LOCUST

DAVID CUNNINGHAM
ANDREW WEATHERALL
TRACEY EMIN
THE APHEX TWIN
WORMHOLE
KEITH BALL
MASSIVE ATTACK
DAVID TOOP
DAMIEN HIRST
ENO
CORNERSHOP
STOCKHAUSEN &
WALKMAN
SAVAGE PENCIL

OVER TO YOU

ROOT
THURSTON MOORE

ALL CONTRIBUTORS WILL RECEIVE A ROYALTY PAYMENT OF 50% OF THE NET PROFIT
SPLIT WITH THURSTON AND DIVIDED BY THE NUMBER OF PARTICIPANTS. ALL PUBLISHING
RIGHTS WILL BE RETAINED BY THE ARTISTS. ALL CONTRIBUTIONS TO BE RECEIVED BY
JAN '98. FOR FURTHER INFORMATION/CONFIRMATION PLEASE PHONE/FAX JON TYE ON
0173 247 2920 OR KEITH BALL ON 0173 382 9031. (PLEASE LET US KNOW ONE WAY OR
ANOTHER IF YOU WISH TO PARTICIPATE).

SILVERSMITHING & J

PRODUCT DESIG

PHOTOGR

GRA

◀ OPEN DESIGN

to: Vilnius Graphic Art Centre
Gallery Kaire-Desine
Latako str. 3
2001 Vilnius, LITHUANIA

from - to: 22.11.2000 - 12.12.2000
tue - fri 11 - 18 | sat 12 - 15 | sun & mon closed

from: Lahti Polytechnic
Institute of Design
Lahti, FINLAND

Artist
The Ark

Title
Calleth You,
Cometh I

24HR CD cover

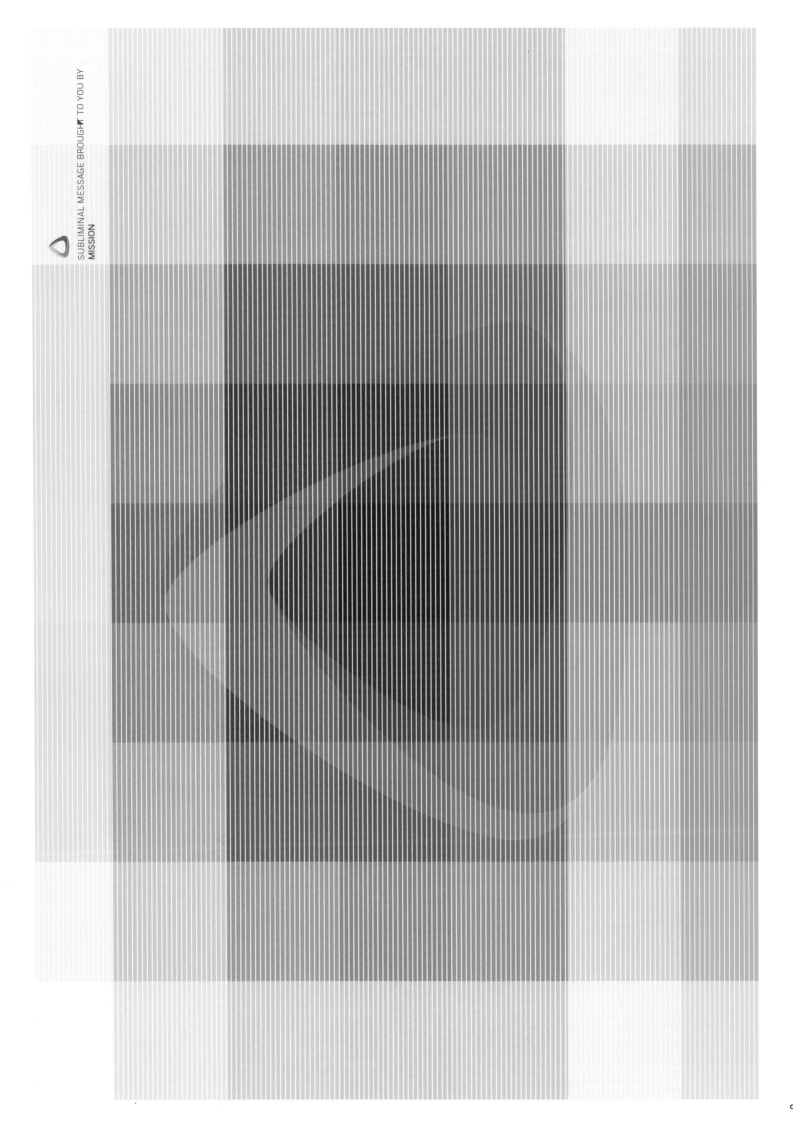

SUBLIMINAL MESSAGE BROUGHT TO YOU BY
MISSION

MISSION Selfpromotion - card

SUBLIMINAL MESSAGE BROUGHT TO YOU BY
MISSION

MISSION T-SHIRT

MISSION BAG

SNOWBOARD

MISSION CAP

MISSION T-SHIRT

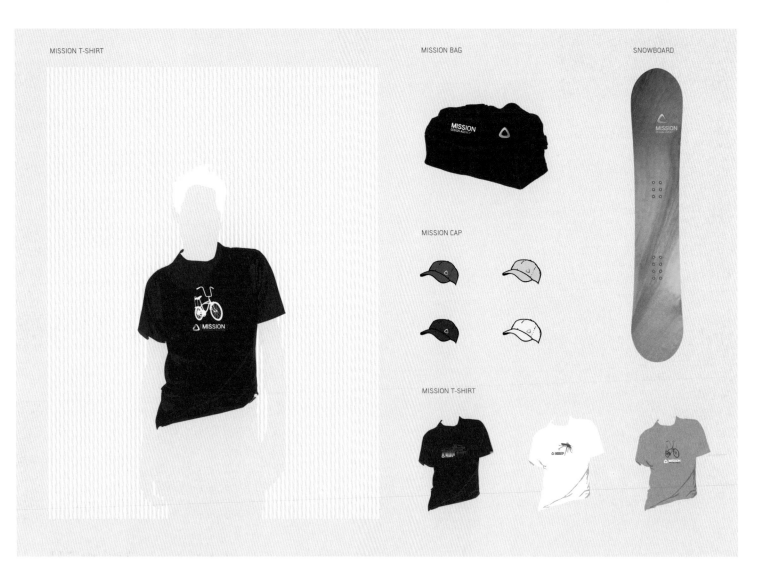

MAIN SYMBOL

SYMBOL VARIATIONS

LOGOTYPE & SUB-REFERENCES

MISSION

MISSION
DESIGN AGENCY

MDA
EST:
2.01

COLOURS

SYMBOL COLOUR VARIATIONS

MISSION FONT

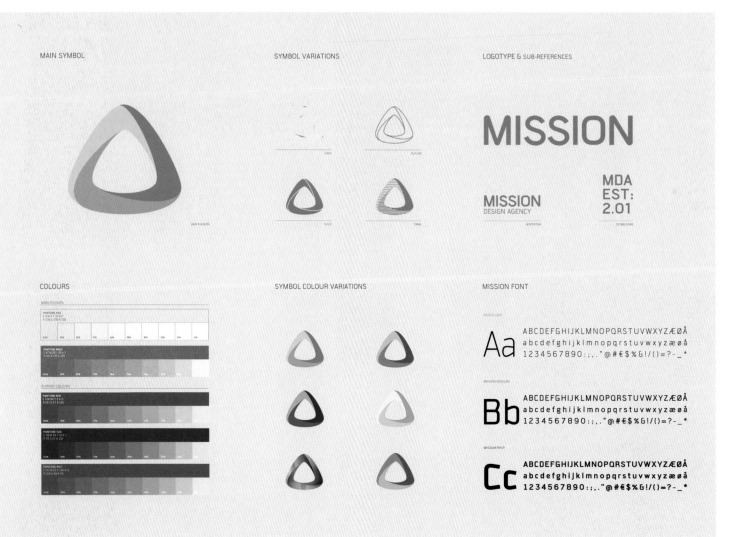

Aa ABCDEFGHIJKLMNOPQRSTUVWXYZÆØÅ
abcdefghijklmnopqrstuvwxyzæøå
1234567890:;,."@#€$%&!/()=?-_*

Bb ABCDEFGHIJKLMNOPQRSTUVWXYZÆØÅ
abcdefghijklmnopqrstuvwxyzæøå
1234567890:;,."@#€$%&!/()=?-_*

Cc ABCDEFGHIJKLMNOPQRSTUVWXYZÆØÅ
abcdefghijklmnopqrstuvwxyzæøå
1234567890:;,."@#€$%&!/()=?-_*

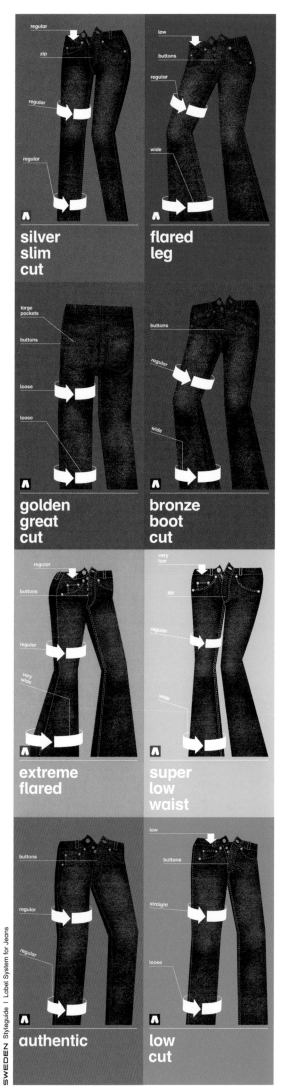

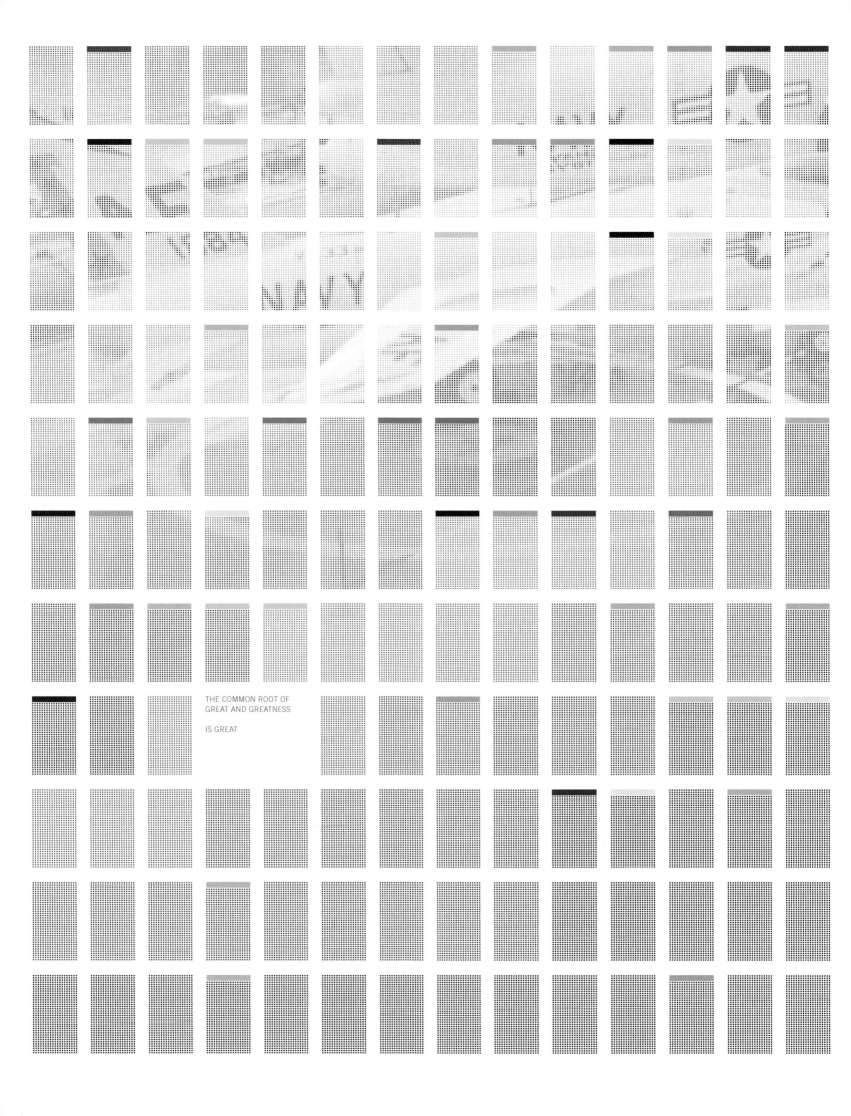

THE COMMON ROOT OF
GREAT AND GREATNESS

IS GREAT

THE DIFFERENCE BETWEEN
GREATNESS AND GREAT

IS NESS

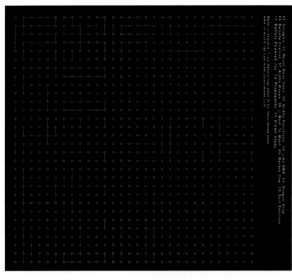

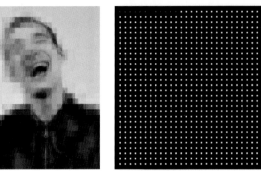

THE BOYS
SING THE
BASSLINE

EB

006

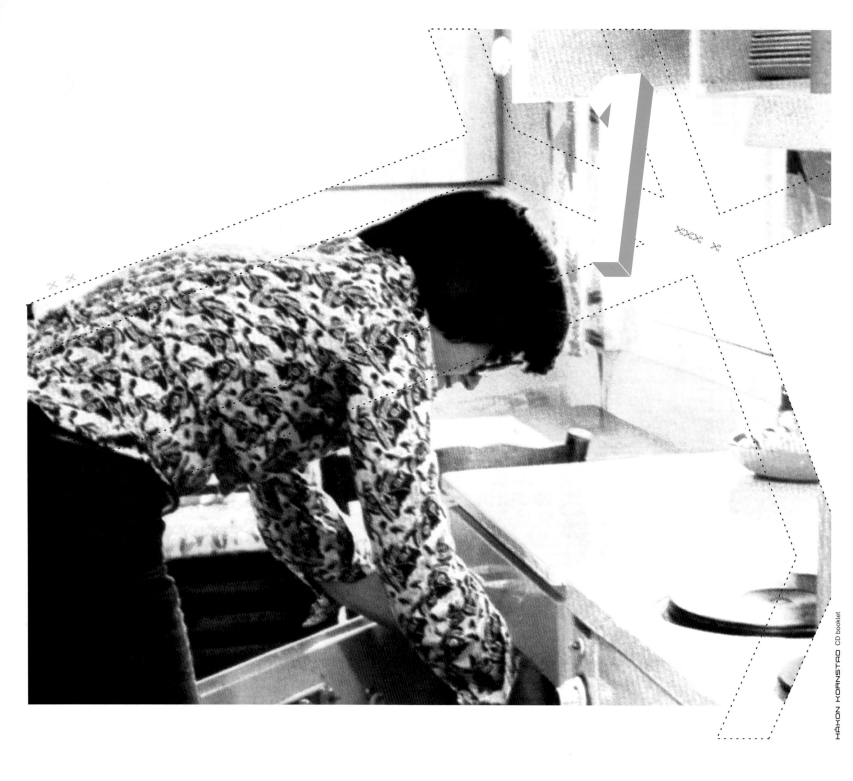

HÅKON KORNSTAD CD booklet

HÅKON KORNSTAD CD booklet

HÅKON KORNSTAD CD booklet

E-TYPES Logo in Cdfé ZORGLOB 2 Images

YOUR THIRST

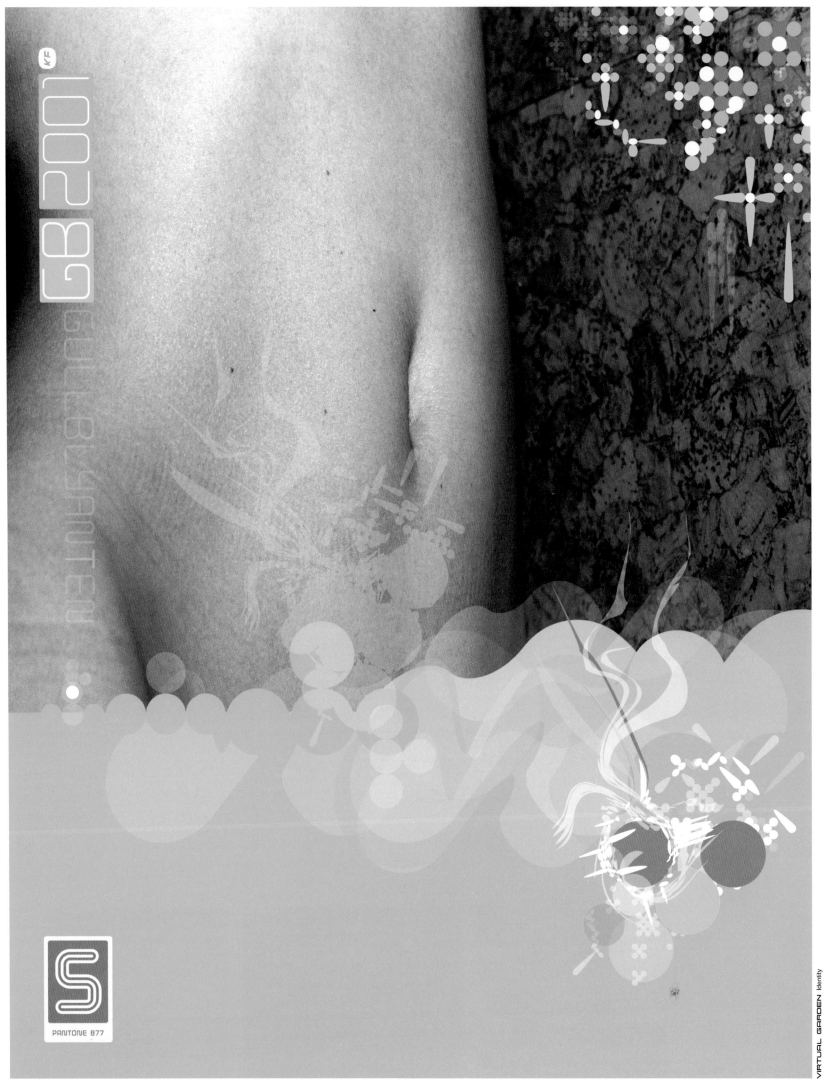

PANTONE 877

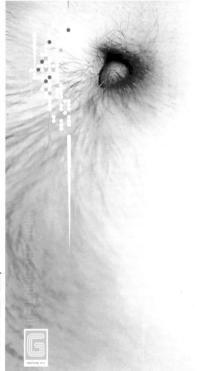

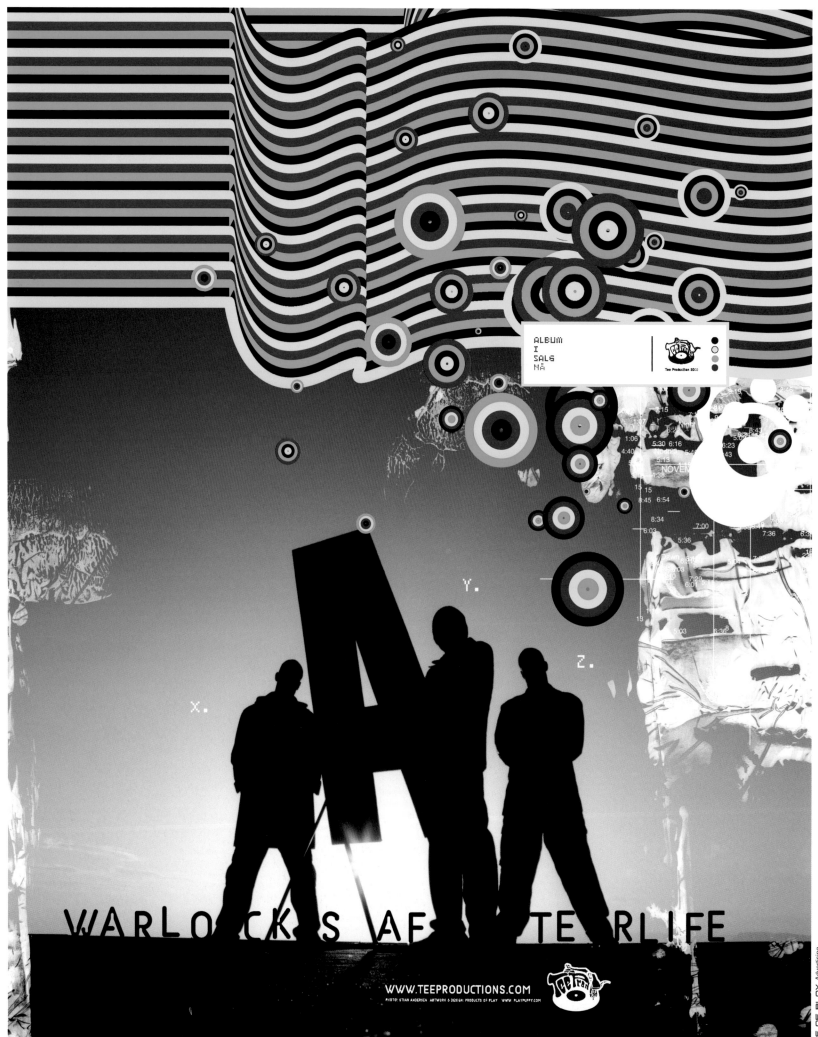

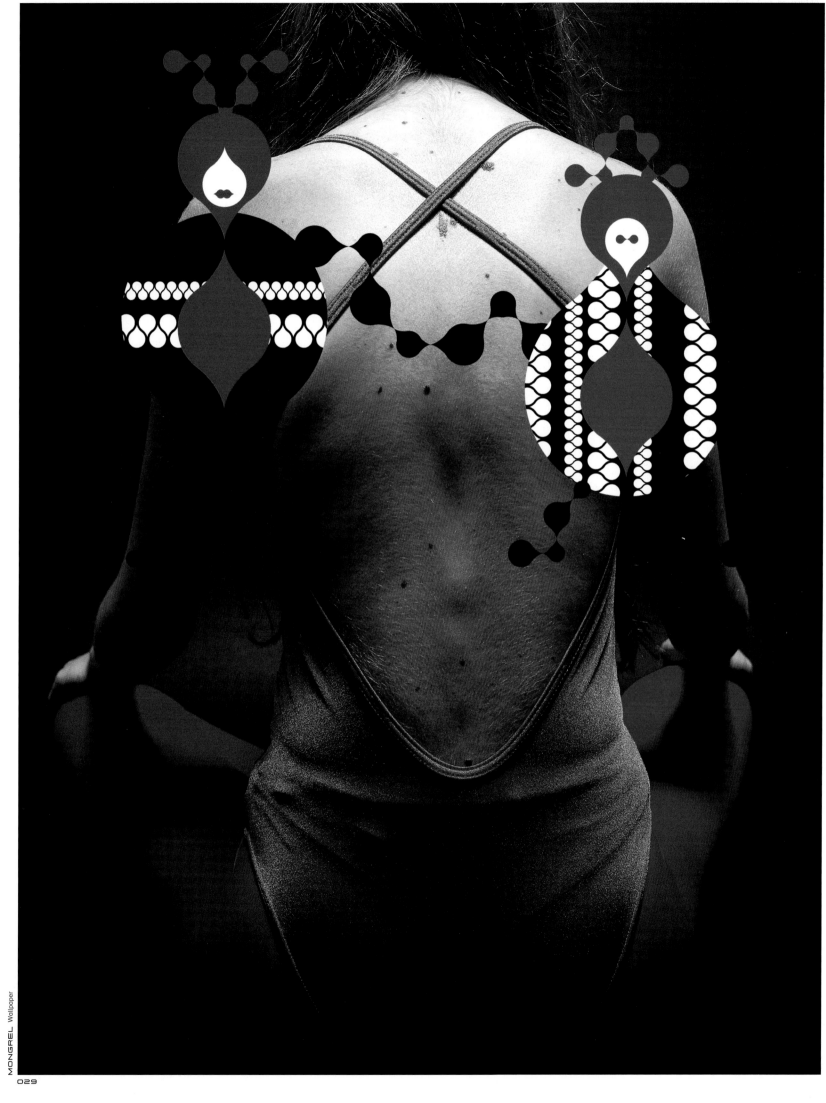

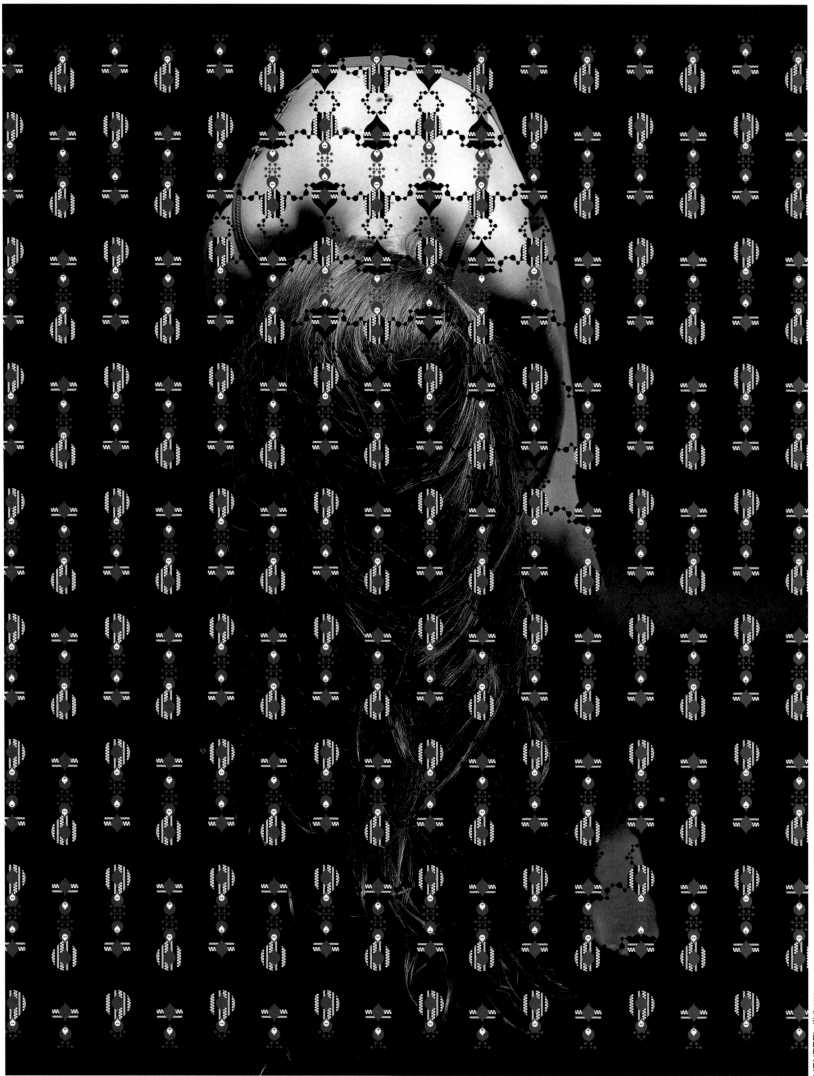

03 SUMMER

Experimental T-shirt collection

Diesel Style Lab
Experimental T-shirt collection

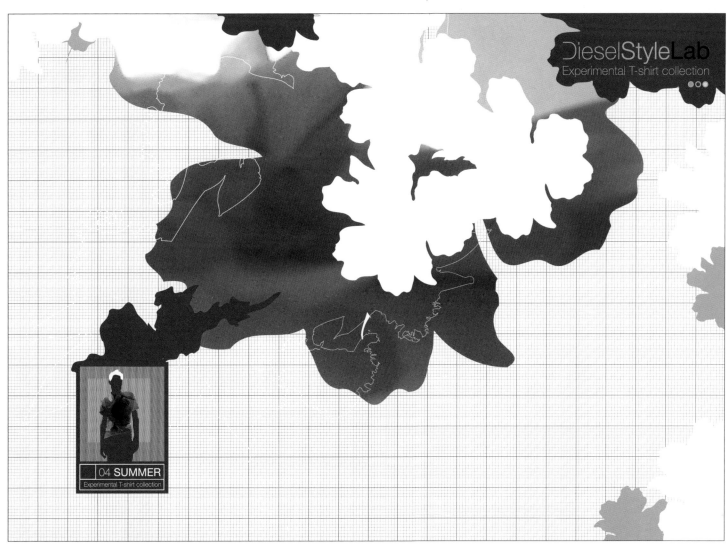

DieselStyleLab
Experimental T-shirt collection

04 SUMMER
Experimental T-shirt collection

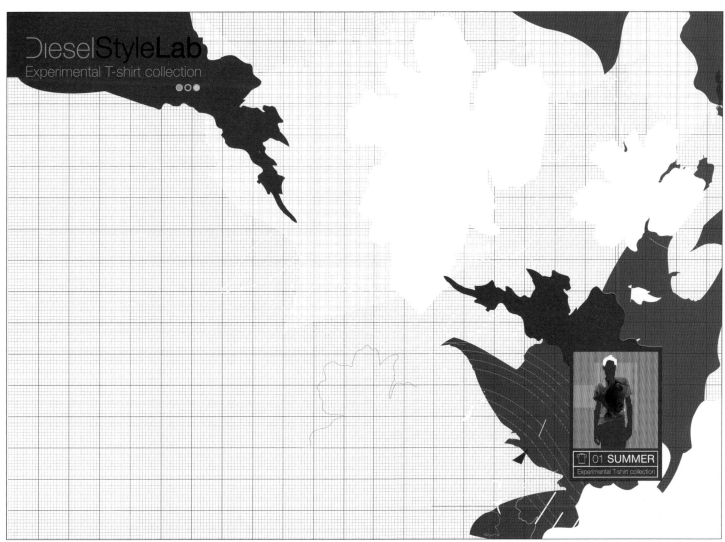

DieselStyleLab
Experimental T-shirt collection

01 SUMMER
Experimental T-shirt collection

Vårsalongen Liljevalchs
25 januari – 17 mars 2002 tisdag – söndag

THE MIND GAME

HECTOR MACDONALD

twins

SWEDEN Interview

Which monkey sat on your back, when you decided to call your company Sweden? Did you run into trouble with the government? **None whatsoever.** I don't really remember how the name came up originally but since then we've decided that Sweden is a good name for us. As a company we are a bit shy, modest and not comfortable with promoting ourselves but underneath we are secretly convinced that we are the best. I think this attitude is somewhat present in the archetypal Swede.

Is there something you really love or hate about Sweden and Scandinavia in general? Personally I don't like the darkness in winter. Other than that I can't think of anything special that makes Sweden attractive or not attractive. There is a lot of open space which is nice, and not a lot of diseases, famine, wars or earthquakes which would threaten to take your mind of the design.

Would you say there is something like a Scandinavian identity of graphic design? And what in particular makes it Scandinavian? I don't think there is anything that is particularly Scandinavian about Scandinavian design but I know that people who have written about us in magazines abroad has described our work as being "typically Northern European", but what that means or how they see it I do not know. I'm often struck by how heterogeneous and faceted all the different Swedish designers are, and I love that. But in instances where people are interested in defining what is Swedish a few qualities are elevated and promoted as being Swedish, and designs made in Sweden carrying those qualities are advertised around the world as being typically " Swedish " . So next time around this " Swedishness" is even more established and pretty soon it becomes a self-reinforcing feedback system. But when I look around I get the feeling that really there is a multitude of different styles and perspectives that are all represented in Sweden by Swedish designers.

Is there a Swedish or Scandinavian design community? Are ideas exchanged by purpose or accident? Are you afraid of copy cats? The organised graphic design community is very weak, if it exists at all. There is not much of a debate going on regarding graphic design. Currently, there are no competent graphic design writers or journalists, but a lot of graphic designers, so in that aspect the community is alive and kicking, but it's my impression that there is less contact with each other than with the "international" design community. I think graphic designers should try to unite because we have no strength when it comes to defending our creative and economic rights to the material we create. Material is used and changed far beyond the intentions of the creator or even the copyright laws, but not much happens and the designer is rarely compensated or respected. Compared with the music industry which has a huge body of interest organisations (Stim, Sami, Gema, Mcps etc.) and ensures that composers are compensated each time their work is used commercially.

Copy cats are a pest - not because they copy your style, but because you start to think your own stuff looks like copies of yourself. I'm finding it harder and harder to do illustrations mainly for this reason. But as a wise man once said: "The imitators are drawn to the imitable", which I interpret along the way of: "If your so good, how come so many are able to copy you?". This is not really a problem and in any case it is not a national problem. The American clothes brand XXXX asked us a couple of years ago to do adverts for them, but we turned them down. Six months later they released ads that at least I thought were a bit too "Sweden". But you can't really complain about stuff like that, half the time you pick up stuff from somewhere else and use it yourself. And in the case of XXXX: they did go through the trouble of contacting us first, that's really all you can ask for I guess.

Scandinavian people seem to care about hipness, are hypes important as an engine for change? Yes, there is a lot of interest in making things look and feel in tune with the zeitgeist. But I think a lot of Swedes are good at cultivating trends as at the same time there is a lot of emphasis on integrity among my colleagues. You can't just copy and paste yourself a reputation. I think the Swedish design culture puts a lot of emphasis on adding your own personality to the work, at least that's how I experience the stuff I see around me.

How did the web influence you? I don't think the web, or stuff on the web influences us a lot. But on the other hand I don't really know what does. We have been asked to write something for a(nother) book on the future of graphic design and we wrote that the most important impact of the internet on the design community is that a lot of (mostly younger) people have started to understand what graphic design is, and can be, through the work with their own and other web sites. When I was in high school I couldn't name even one typeface. Today I think the situation is different. It's my belief that this development is the single most important factor that will make graphic design an even more influential part of culture than it is today.

You have a social/political approach in many of your designs. Especially your works for Dr. Kosmos (a Swedish pop band) reflect and illustrate their clever lyrics perfectly. Do you think that you stand alone with this attitude? And does this clash with your work for the Erikson mobile phone group or H&M? Hard to tell, we are definitely the ones who put that flag down first, but like all trends they appear at many different places at the same time. And as soon as things get trendy the initial intention can get lost very quickly. At this point in time it's hard to tell if there's anything more behind the Che Guevara faces and stretched fists. I'm not even sure what made us go down that path in the first place, the ambition to be righteous or the ambition to be cool. But in some circles the political awareness or whatever you choose to call it is a trend in itself so that would naturally reflect the design made by people involved in it.

As a designer I think there is a kind of morale that tells you to get involved and change whatever you can on whatever level you are allowed to. A drive to make design as good and competent as you can and at the same time try to squeeze in your outlook on society if possible. When we did the neck labels for H&M (which now display the size of the garments big and clearly), one of the comments was that girls are afraid to reveal their sizes or are reluctant to wear clothes with a clearly visible size. We answered that even if that's true, that's a kind of perspective that we don't want to include in our design, and through taking things like that into consideration is a soft way of accepting it,

which we don't. We also said that H&M shouldn't care to much about things like that, as it might actually reinforce the phenomena at the same time. And in the end they respected that which felt good and was, in my opinion, pretty brave on their side. But the bottom line is that as a graphic designer you are a gun for hire and the design world is a commercial world. We want to do as much design as we can for as many clients possible, as long as the assignments are stimulating and the clients are prepared to accept the designers' point of view. This is really the single most important factor in choosing our clients – to have a good feeling about the client and a feeling that you will be able (and that they will allow you) to do something good, no matter if it's a rock band or a multinational company. Some people have told us that we lose credibility by working for H&M, but I think that when it comes down to it, it has more to do with the fact that H&M sells cheap clothes and will never have the same credibility as a company that sells expensive clothes, rather than the fact that H&M is a big commercial enterprise. For the same reason H&M is often seen as a more "evil" company than upmarket companies, but if you believe that you are the biggest marketing victim of all.

If you want to change the world at least a bit by your design, what is your master plan? I think our design is sort of harmless and in its best moments fun and clever in a serious way which I think is a nice way to communicate things as opposed to be too cool or detached or visually violent. If anything, I hope that we inspire people to follow our path.

Is Scandinavian design sexy? Do you have design groupies? Just last month we got an invitation to be in a book about sex in graphic design and we realised that we haven't done anything that can be perceived as sexy and there are not a lot of sassy girls or nudity in our work. Sex and the use of sexuality is perhaps not the strongest point in Swedish design. Especially not for "shock value", and I think in general Swedes regard it as a bit cheap and unsophisticated to use "sexy" material like that. We have to make our point in other ways to be taken seriously. As for groupies ...no, apart from a single incident by Australian girls, all the appreciation we get is cheerful, sober "fan mail". As I said earlier my impression is that a lot of younger people today are aware that there are designers behind every CD cover, book jacket etc. and, if they like what they see, they will take their time to seek out whoever that is instead of just telling the band or the author.

What sets your personal work apart from your commercial projects? To date I've never experienced any work being more personal or commercial than any other. The final application might be different, but while you are actually working with it you just want to achieve the best solution for that particular situation, the feeling is exactly the same. But of course the "purpose" when doing some kinds of commercial work is more clearly defined, which can affect the way you work. As I mentioned earlier, the whole point with being a designer is that you are "commercial" i.e. doing something in a context decided or created by someone else (which doesn't necessarily mean you're getting paid!). My experience is that in general all good designers' "personal" or "experimental" work is totally pointless, or at best not as interesting as their commercial work. Pretty much in the same way that when talented fine artists are asked to work with companies or advertising campaigns. The interesting quality is lost in some way. It seems to me that a lot of design and/or art is interesting just BECAUSE it is used in a commercial (or a non-commercial) context. You need that kind of "tension" that the context creates to perceive the quality in design or art.

What influences the process coming up with an idea? Just the aesthetics or also a possible message/interpretation? I'm having problems with working with aesthetics only, which doesn't mean that I think it's wrong. When working I just feel the need to use ideas or say something at the same time. It is the result of the way you judge the quality of your own work. But the pure decorative side of design is coming on strong in the wonderful world of graphic design and for Nando Costa's Brazil project we've done a series of wallpaper designs which are meant to be more decorative than fun or smart. That felt really fresh to work with.

What would you do if graphic design didn't exist? Invent it. ...Sorry, what a lame answer. We don't have a clear idea what would be going on then.

Do the landscapes/dark winters/midsummer nights have an effect on your soul and design? I get easily depressed during the winter with so few daylight hours, but on the other hand I have a lot more problems concentrating on work during the summer months. The autumn and winter months can get pretty creative and productive which is a good thing. And I think a lot of Swedes have an idea that when the autumn comes it's time to get started again whilst the summer months are a sort of carefree release. I guess this sort of cycle can be pretty healthy for your mind. Last month I was in Germany showing some sketches and the client thought our work was very much influenced by Ingmar Bergman but I was too afraid to ask what they meant. Maybe there is something heavy and gloomy about us Swedes even when we try to colour it 100% magenta.

What influence does traditional folkloristic art and pop art have on your work? Pop art has influenced the visual climate so much that it is not even an influence anymore. I don't see that as an isolated influence on what we do, but of course it's there somewhere. One thing that the Pop Art movement did do was that it highlighted the aesthetic qualities in commercially created graphics which in the long run probably helped people see the beauty of "everyday" graphics. For me personally I've come to realise that my childhood home, filled to the limit with South American art and crafts has probably laid the foundation to what I like today, in the way of appreciating strong colours, patterns etc.

What would you do if you weren't a designer? Is there maybe an electronic pop project to stop you from going crazy over design? I would probably open a pet store and Magnus would play badminton 24-7. Right now it is mostly design that occupies our minds. We recently became partial owners of a publishing company and that felt like a good way to broaden our activities, and YES there are rumours about a band...

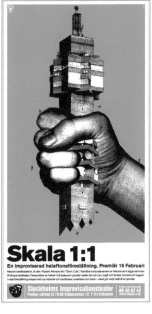

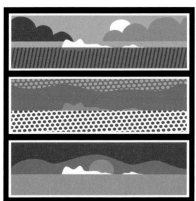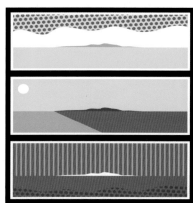

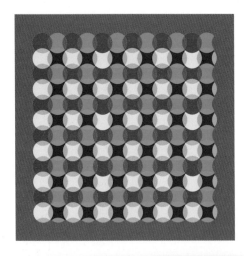
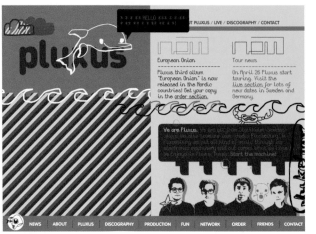

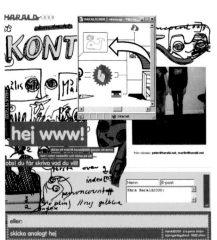

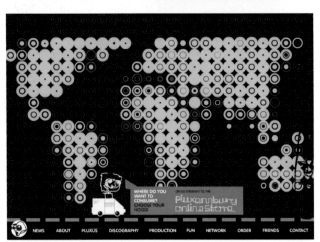

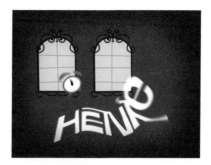

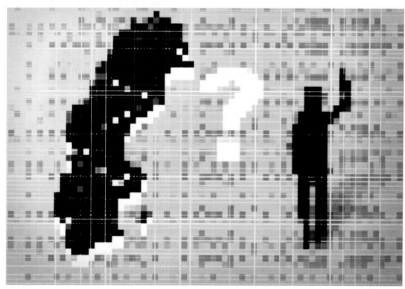

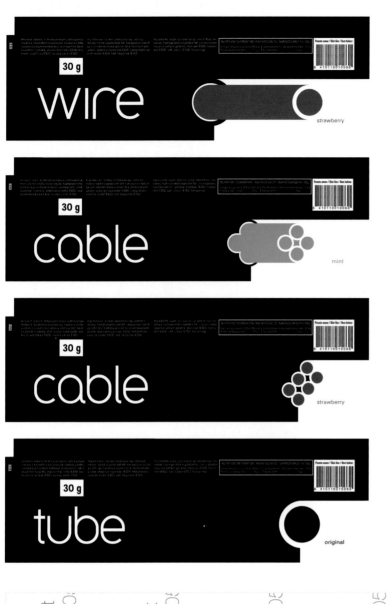

30 g

wire

strawberry

30 g

cable

mint

30 g

cable

strawberry

30 g

tube

original

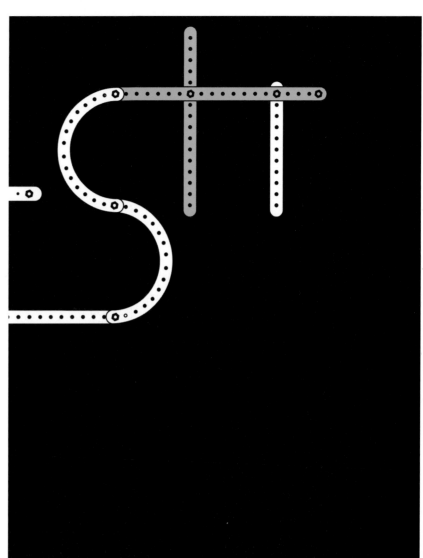

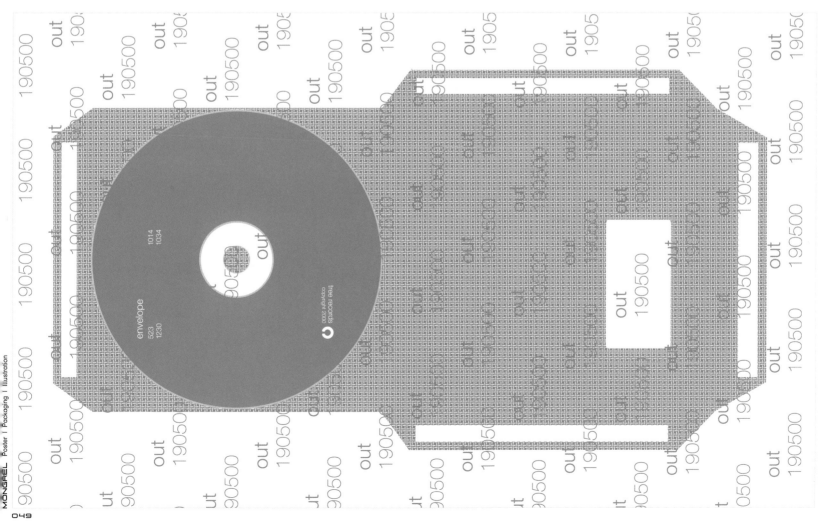

envelope
523
1230

1014
1034

tree records
copyright 2000

out 190500

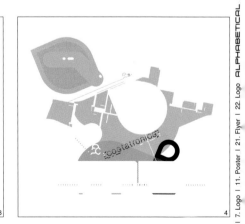

222 *NEW YORK* 222

ELECTROCLASH

RESPECT PER FRONTH

13

WETWARE

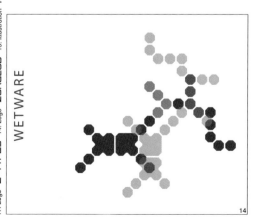

14

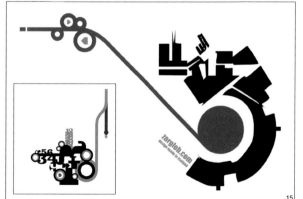

15

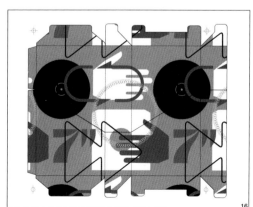

16

17

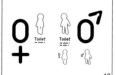

18

19

20

21

22

23

24

håkan lidbo
before the beginning

håkan lidbo
after the end

ABCDEFGHIJKLMNOPQRSTUVWXYZÆØ 0123456789

CLEANFAX

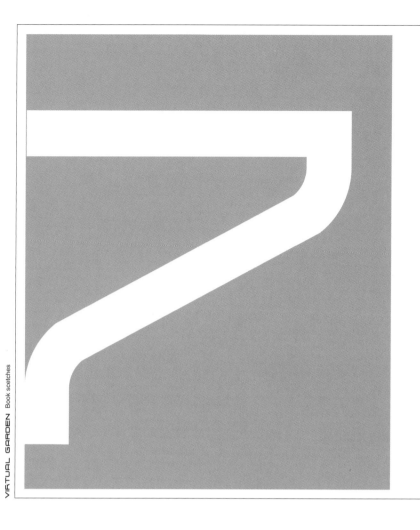

VIRTUAL GARDEN Book scetches

det tapte

PARADIS

MONGREL Logo typeface

PIA WALL / STAVANGERILLUSTRATØRENE Security symbols

SUBTOPIA CD cover

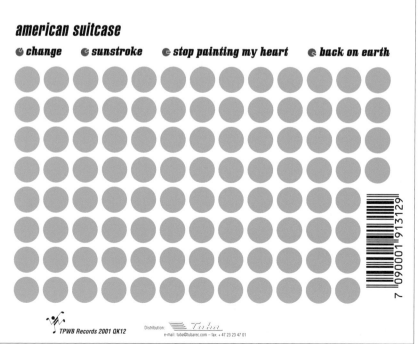

american suitcase

● *change* ● *sunstroke* ● *stop painting my heart* ● *back on earth*

TPWB Records 2001 QK12

Distribution: *Tuba*
e-mail: tuba@tubarec.com — fax: + 47 23 23 47 01

7 090001 913129

american suitcase ★

Thatsperfectwonderball Records

"*change*"

053

MUCK

while | I'm | gone

DA BOOK

ONE
TABOO
TO

1

2

3

4

5

8

6

7

9

VDGNMAGERGADE 10
DK-1120 KØBENHAVN K

TELEFON/ +45 3374 3400
TELEFAX/ +45 3374 3401
E-MAIL/ JOURNAL@DFI.DK

DET DANSKE FILMINSTITUT

DET DANSKE FILMINSTITUT
VIRKSOMHEDSREGNSKAB 1998

E-TYPES Catalogue cover

FACE IT

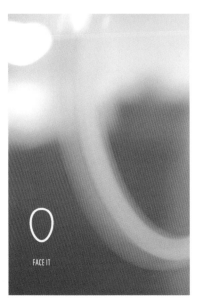

Function follows form
www.greyscale.net

SUPERLOW Dezine 3 VIRTUAL GARDEN Identity GREYSCALE Image

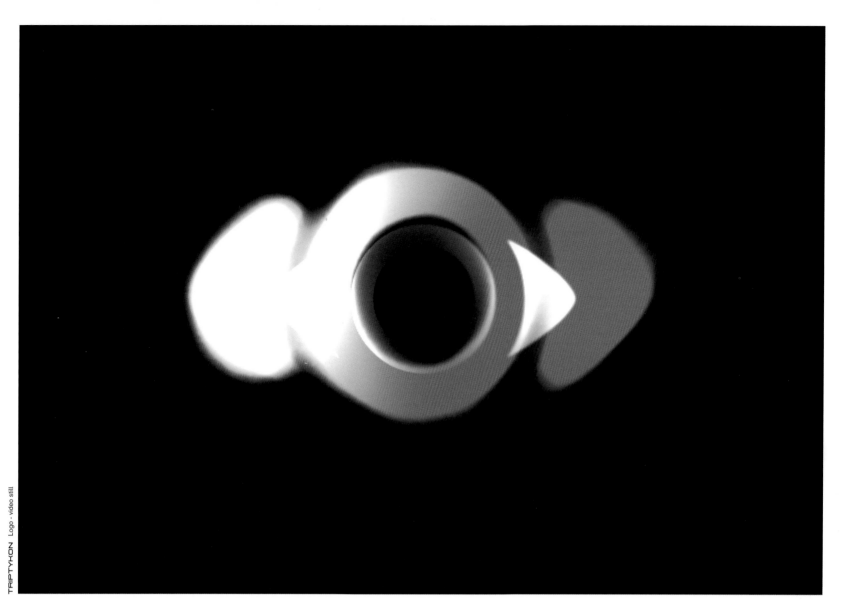

TRIPTYKON Logo · video still

E-TYPES Catalogue cover · TRIPTYKON Christmas card

www.framfab.com/jobs

framfab ▶▶

FramFab CultureMag™
No. 51 2000

formula

GLÆDELIG JUL 2001

057

LOST WAYS

JARVIS
SWEET
PARSONS
BIGS

WAYS

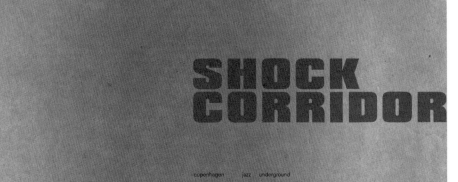

SHOCK
CORRIDOR

copenhagen   jazz   underground

FORBIDDEN FRUIT
LOST WAYS

JARVIS
SWEET
PARSONS
BIGS

LOST P WAYS

JARVIS
SWEET
PARSONS
DUO

INCOMMUNICADO

copenhagen   jazz   underground

NEW
PLANET®

FIRMA
blackout 3:01 / via blood 19:39 / old thing 2:13

kresten jessen: tenor saxophone, ejvin nordström: guitar and rune folkert: bass
recorded live at The Fruit Cellar; march 3rd 2002

NEW DUO
now you don't 3:51 / henderson 9:29 / anymore 2:13

mikkel holm: cornet and stefan hivert: guitar and bass
recorded live at The Fruit Cellar; december 23rd 2003

ENDLESS QUARTET
nothing 11:10 / beat 3:20 / mama 4:08

anders nielsen: saxophones, robert mortensen: trumpet and synthesizers
erland mikkelberg: bass and julian wees: drums
recorded live at The Fruit Cellar; january 1st 2002

konstruktion, 123 broadway 10th fl. new york, ny 10010

copenhagen   underground   jazz
tomorrow's milky ways

THE UNIT
BIG
CHILL

THE UNIT
MOVE ANY
MOUNTAIN

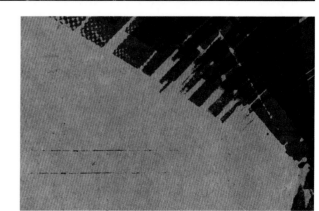

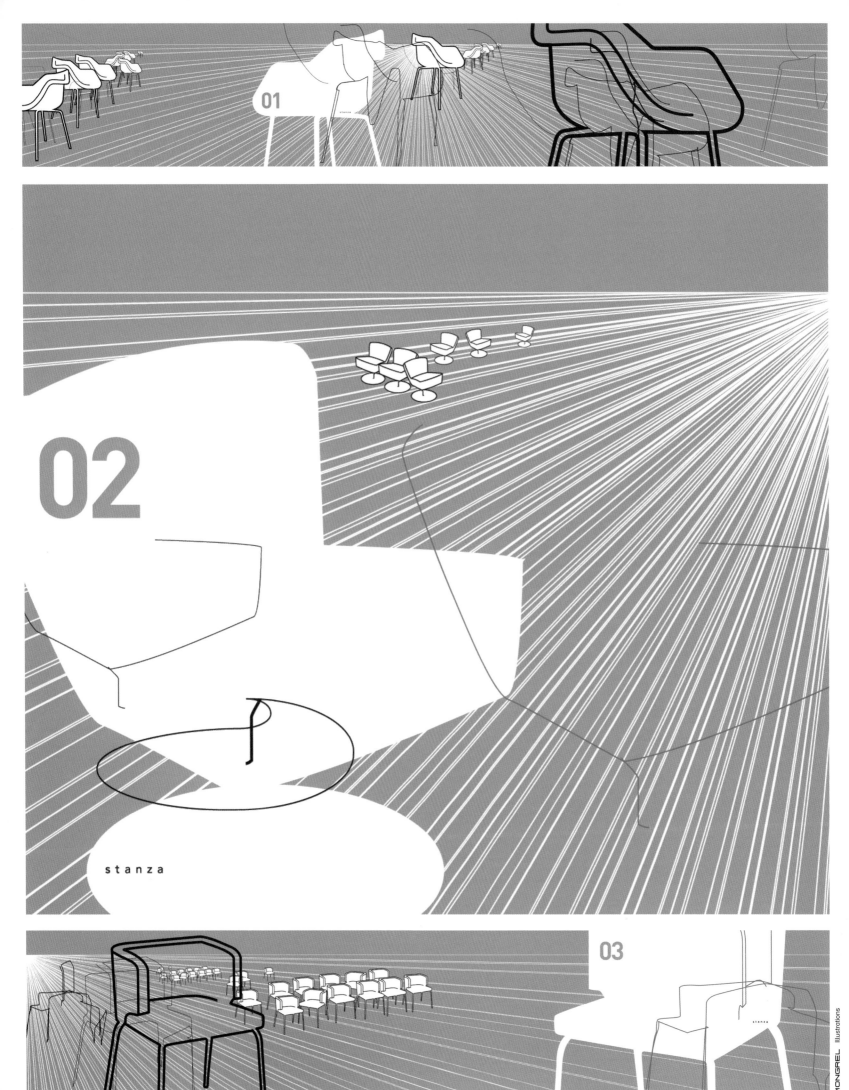

01

02

stanza

03

MONGREL Illustrations

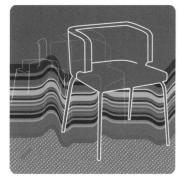

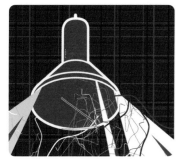

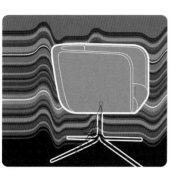

hellestø strand søndag 3 juni klokken 13

dragefesten 2001

TA MED DRAGE, NISTEKURV OG VINDJAKKE OG BLI MED PÅ NORGES STØRSTE DRAGEFESTIVAL.
PREMIER, DIPLOMER, SALG AV DRAGER OG GODTERIER. PARKERING KR 20.
BYGG DIN EGEN DRAGE MED SOLA DRAGEKLUBB I SOLA KULTURHUS LØRDAG 2 JUNI KL 11-15.
ARR. SOLA DRAGEKLUBB, HAVDUR OG SOLA KULTURKONTOR.

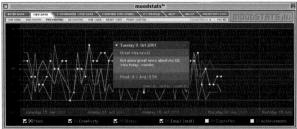
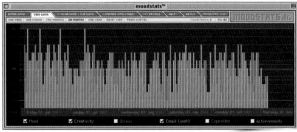

SCANDINAVIAN WEB DESIGN

When we were asked to write this feature, our immediate reaction was, "Is there such a thing as Scandinavian Web Design?" And even after having spent long nights pondering upon that very subject, we were still not sure. How can you take the vast variety of design styles, subject matter, and execution found in this book and throw it all together into one easily definable category?

The awkward urge to categorise and label certain 'schools' of design often results in overly simplistic and crude equations. Take the notion of 'Swiss Design', for example. To many people, Swiss design IS Joseph Müller-Brockmann; to them he is the epitome of everything flat, economically designed and typographically superior. But sadly forgotten are other highly influential designers and design ideas like the post-war styles of Armin Hofman and the candy-coloured works of Wolfgang Weingart. Shaping Swiss Design was, and still is, not a one-man exercise and the same applies to Scandinavian design.

Sure enough, we, too, have our holy cows: the old masters of furniture design and architecture, the ones that everybody outside of Scandinavia feel are "typically Danish", "typically Swedish", "typically Finnish" even. But when it comes to the web, the style and approach of Scandinavian design is ever so multifarious - from the use of materials and media to the inspiration and application.

While flicking through the pages of North by North, much to our surprise, we suddenly found ourselves muttering, "sure - you can smell the Nordic flavour from miles away". It seemed that Scandinavian designers share some common traits; the functional, often rigid and grid-like structure, the lavish use of white space to evoke an atmosphere and focus the eyes on one single design element, the love of beautiful, timeless photography and illustration, the kitsch, the lines, the squares, the slightly obsessive attention to all the minor details and last, but not least, the tongue-in-cheek humour – dry, understated, and without the crass edge often found amongst our American brethren.

In order to understand, however, why we would consider these elements to be hallmarks of the Scandinavian design style, one would have to take a step back and look at Scandinavian culture in general. Scandinavians are metropolitan by nature and have always been extremely open and receptive to all kinds of foreign influences. There is

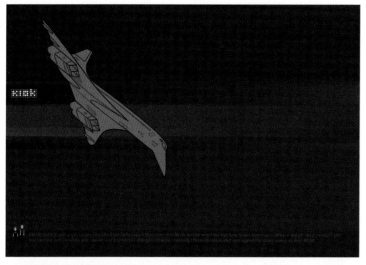

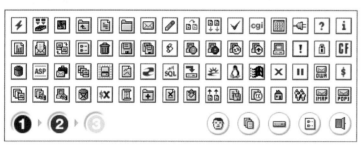

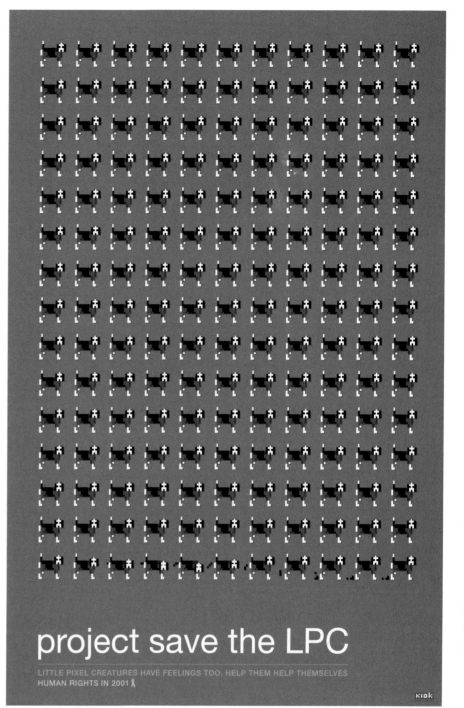

project save the LPC

LITTLE PIXEL CREATURES HAVE FEELINGS TOO. HELP THEM HELP THEMSELVES
HUMAN RIGHTS IN 2001

a great fondness for everything American and British, but also an awareness of other European, Asian and South American trends. Being such small nations, they put a huge effort into educating the population about the rest of the world, and learning 2-3 foreign languages at an early age is not unusual. Scandinavians tend to travel a lot, and usually have no problems immersing themselves in the cultures of countries far, far away.

The landscape and climate, along with the often restrictive and bland political system, encourages the daydreaming mentality. Inspiration seems to come easily to the lone Scandi, spending long, gray winter days in his semi-detached wooden house in the middle of nowhere. This is probably the same oppressive dullness that made the Vikings embark on their rape and pillaging trips across the world, and in many ways the internet, which is widely used in all the Nordic countries, seems to be the perfect vessel for the modern Scandi to explore, colonize, plunder and reconstruct.

The Scandinavians are masters of merging disparate elements, of understanding the ideas that underlay a given school of design, which also explains the multitude of different influences that can be spotted throughout this book; from Japanese manga madness, the hard grids of the Swiss and simplistic colour usage like Germany's Bauhaus movement to American boldness or the typographic finesse of the Dutch, everything has been thrown together, swirled around and later siphoned off again to produce the great variety of work on display here.

And that, we think, is the beauty of this particular beast. Scandinavian design is like an exquisitely made quilt, where every single patch, a small masterpiece in itself, has been carefully selected based on its ability to blend in with the other patches. It's not a strict mathematical equation, it can't be distilled and bottled; instead, it is a feeling, an ability to take the best from the rest of the world and make it even better, with that added touch of Nordic sauna flavour.

Happy viewing.

mschmidt & token, KALIBER10000

beige
I don't either

BEIGE

A01: NULL TO ZERO A02: MELODRAMATIC SYSTEM ERROR
A03: HYDRO-PORTO A04: YAKUMO DIPPEL A05: BEIGE 03 A06:
RUNKELRUBE BLAU A07: BEIGE 04/35/08
B01: THE GREAT KRAUTROCK SWINDLE B02: ZUBEHD...
B03: JAMAIKA FRAKTAL B04: FREAKY FUCKIN' WIND...
B05: 12 A PRT07-2 B06: REPRO 01/14/04...
18 INCH BLACK B08: MONO TONIC MIT LEG

EKHORNFORSS/NON-FORMAT CD cover

GREYSCALE.NET

- FUNCTION
- FOLLOWS
- FORM

GREYSCALENET Untitled 1 + 2

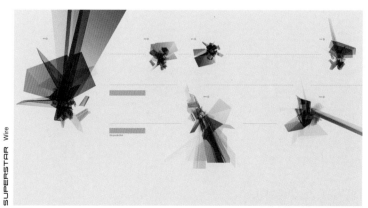

SUPERSTAR Wire

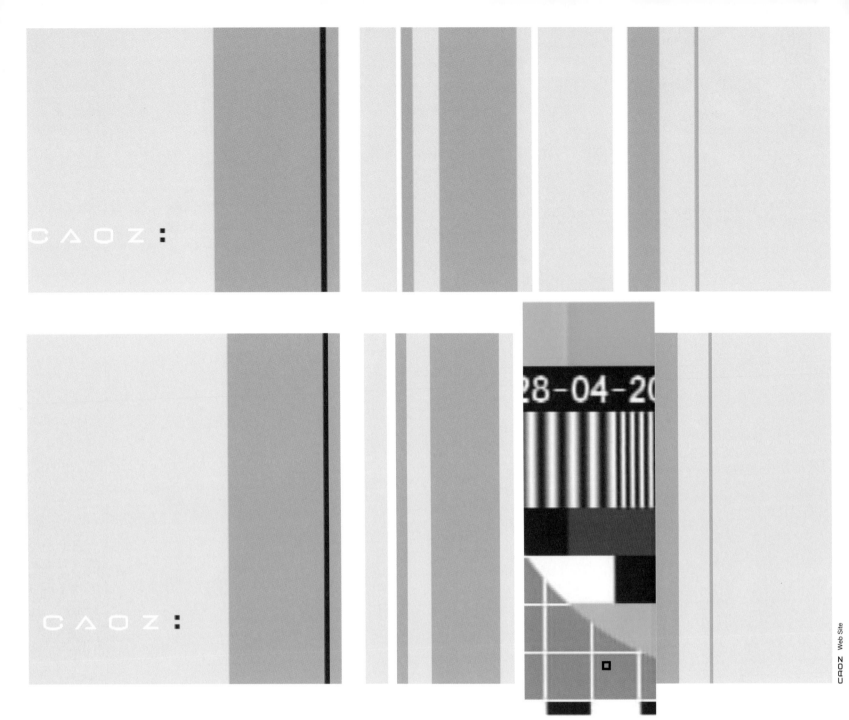

CAOZ Web Site

SUBTOPIA Web site   PEHMUSTE Web site

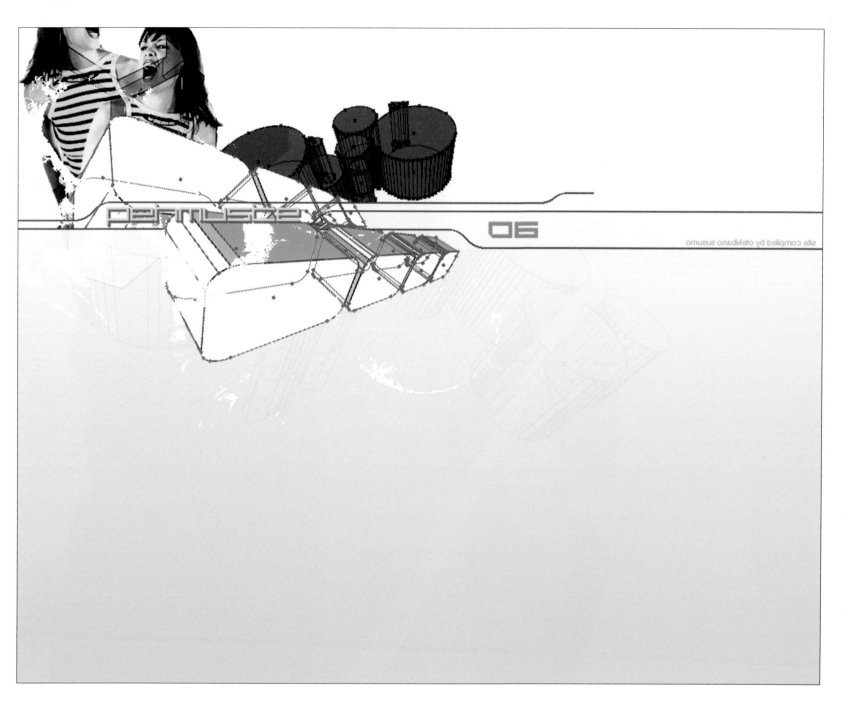

site compiled by otakibano susumo

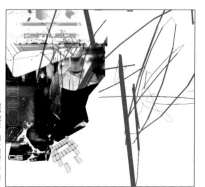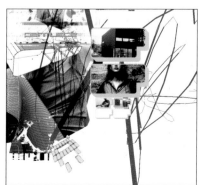

PEH-MJSTE Web site

accept nothing :reject

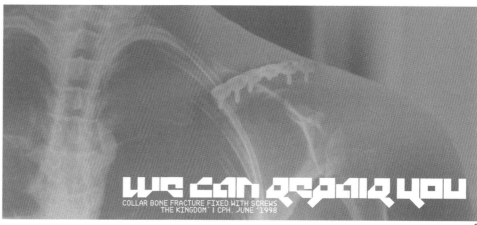

We can repair you

COLLAR BONE FRACTURE FIXED WITH SCREWS
»THE KINGDOM« I CPH. JUNE '1998

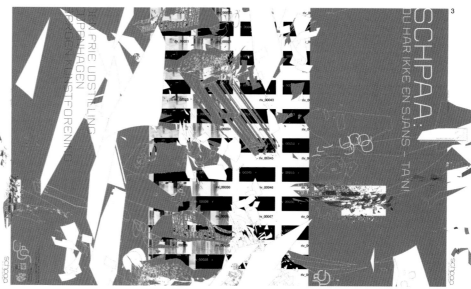

SUPERLOW   1. CD Cover I 3. Catalogue Cover I 4. CD Cover I 7. Dezine 2   SUBTOPIA   5. CD Cover   MONO CYKLON   2. »Repair«   BLEED   7. Untitled

069

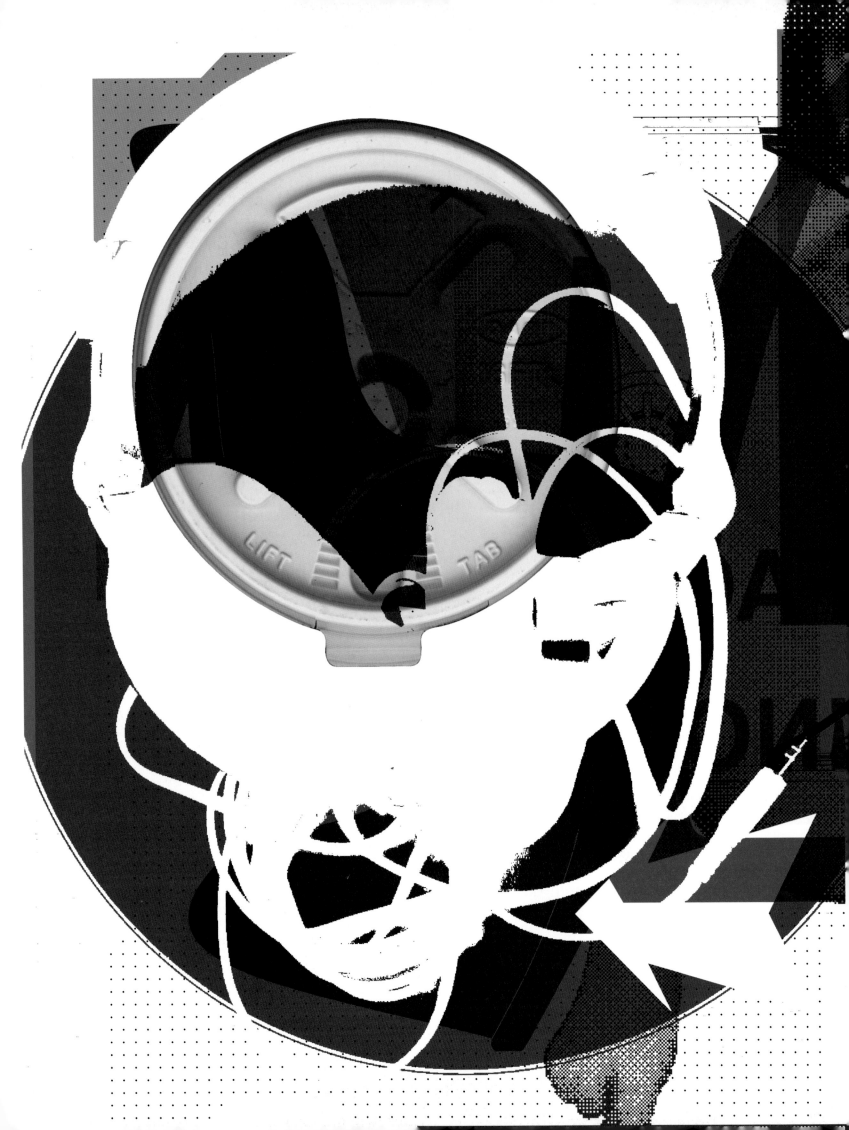

ABC80™

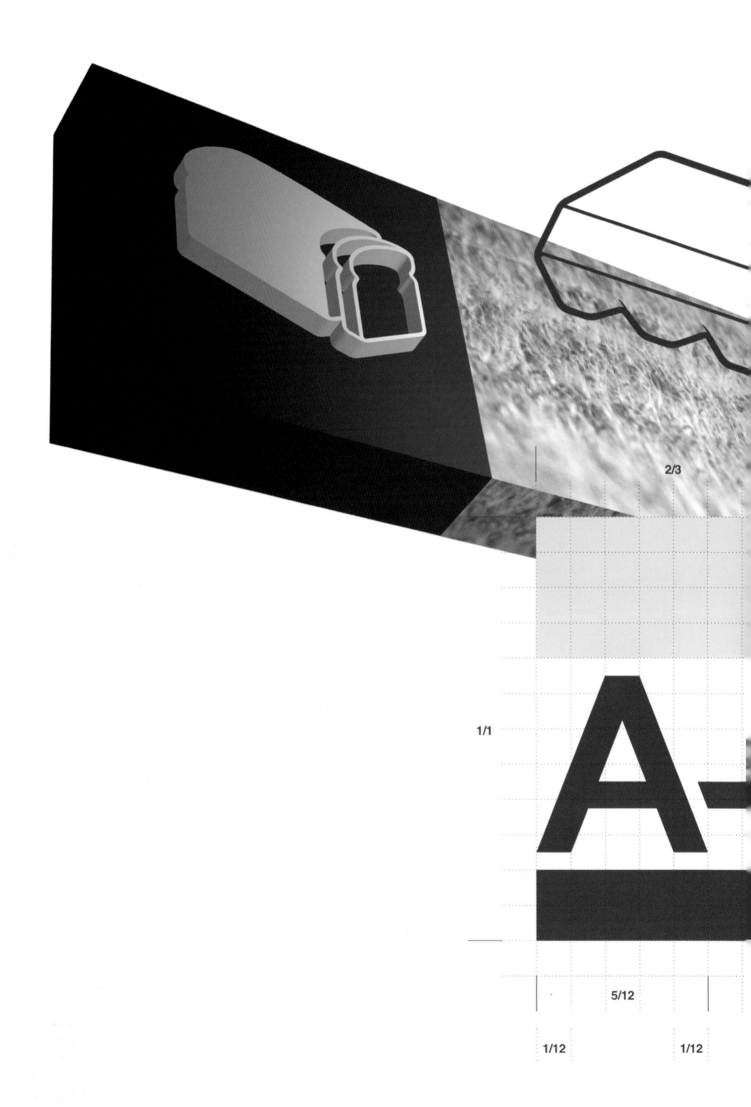

A-

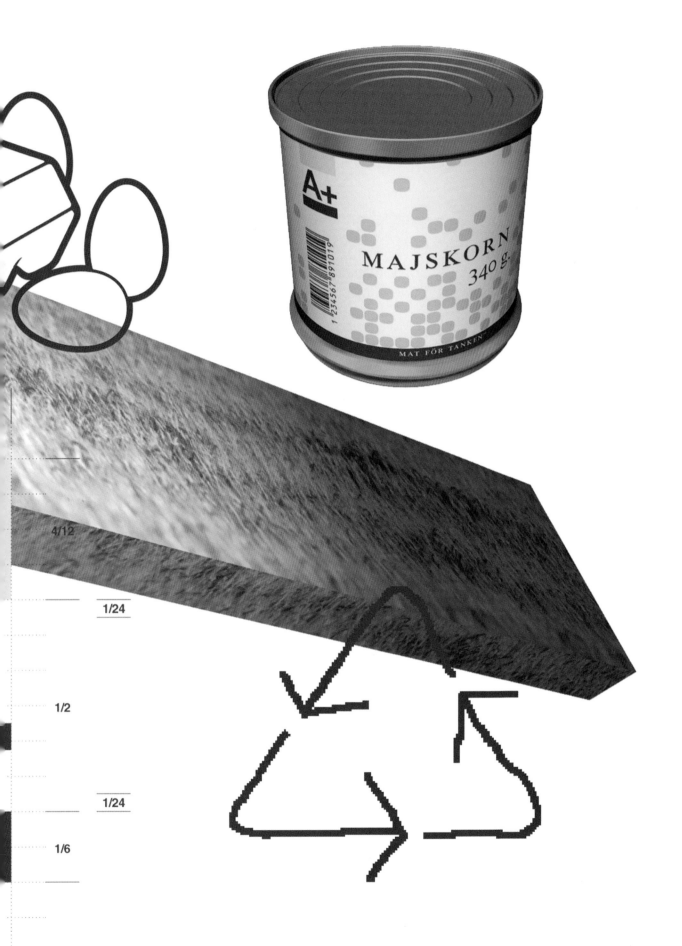

A+

MAJSKORN
340 g.

1 234567 891019

MAT FÖR TANKEN

4/12

1/24

1/2

1/24

1/6

Børn der mobber   behøver kærlighed

den som ikke belæres af sin mor   vil blive belært af verden

HANNE CASSIM Bully

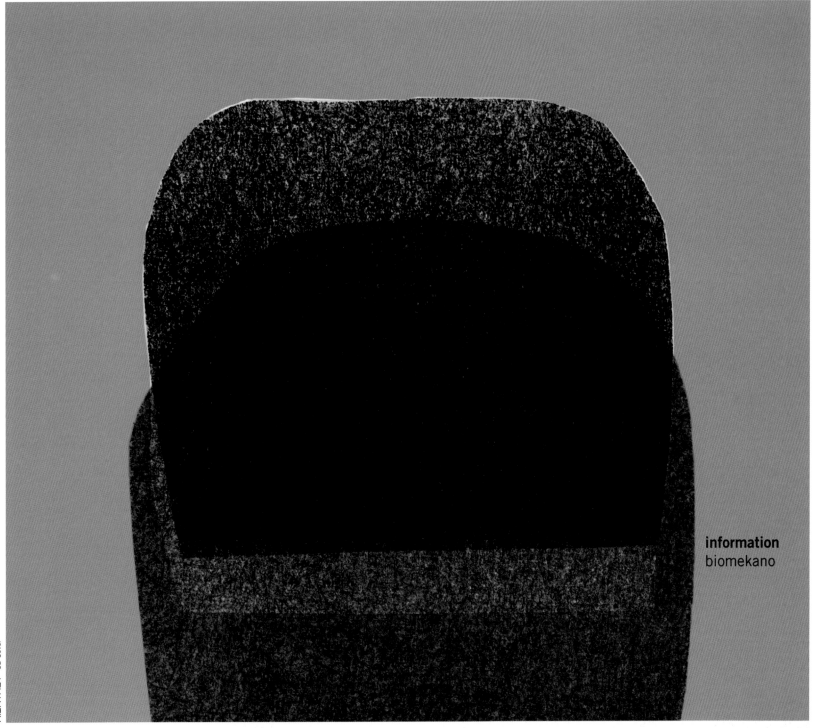

information
biomekano

S   A

Koneisto. Festival for electronic music. July 27th-28th, 2001. Turku, Finland.

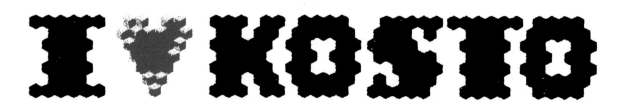

Koneisto. Festival for electronic music. July 27th-28th, 2001. Turku, Finland. More kosto at www.koneisto.com

SYRUP HELSINKI Koneisto Festival 2001 · Slogan · Poster

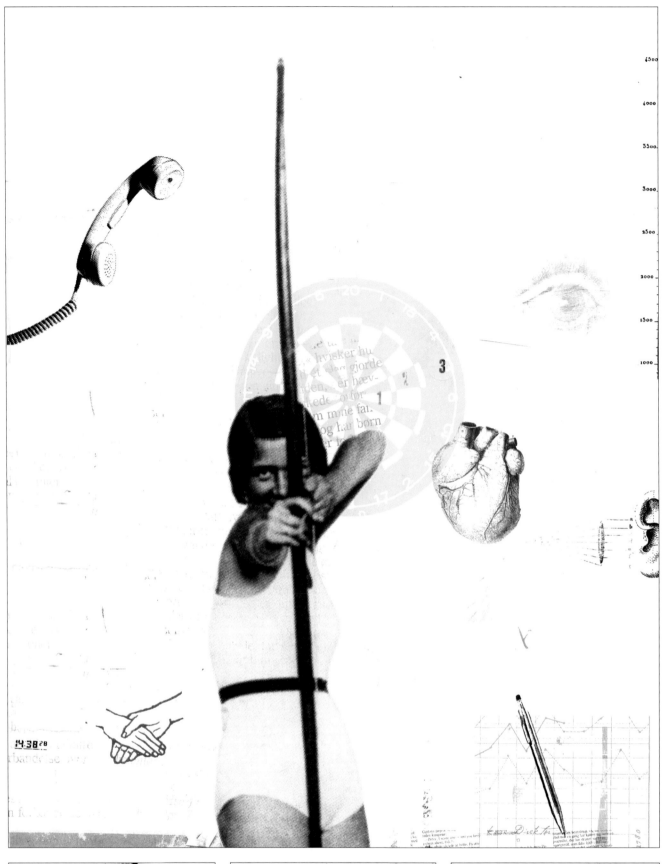

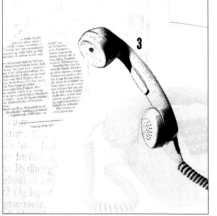
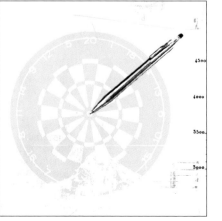

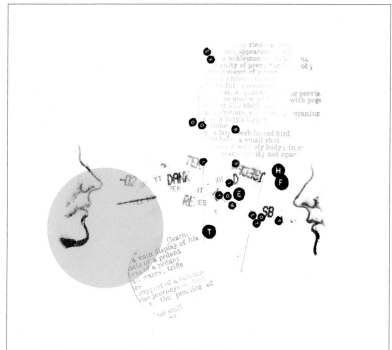

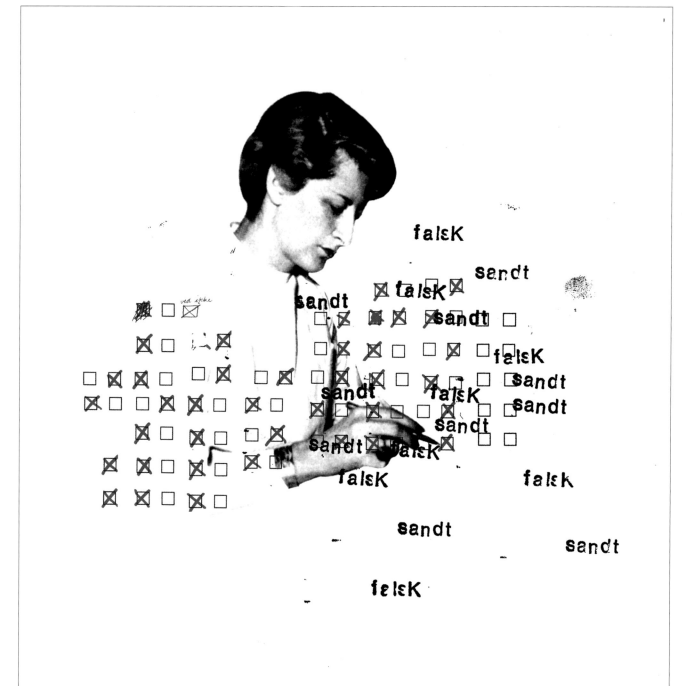

CAMILLA IRMELIN MYKLEBUST / STAVANGERILLUSTRATØRENE »Oil industry«

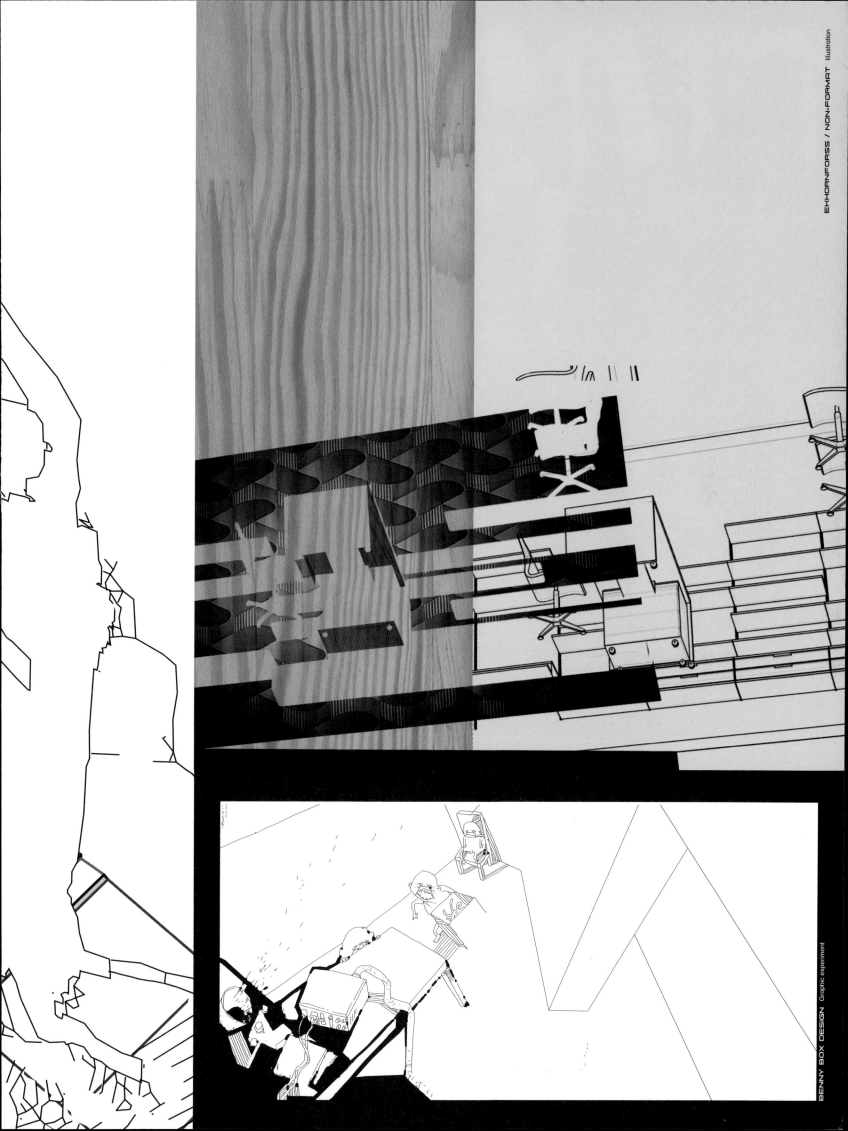

BENNY BOX DESIGN Magazine cover

275

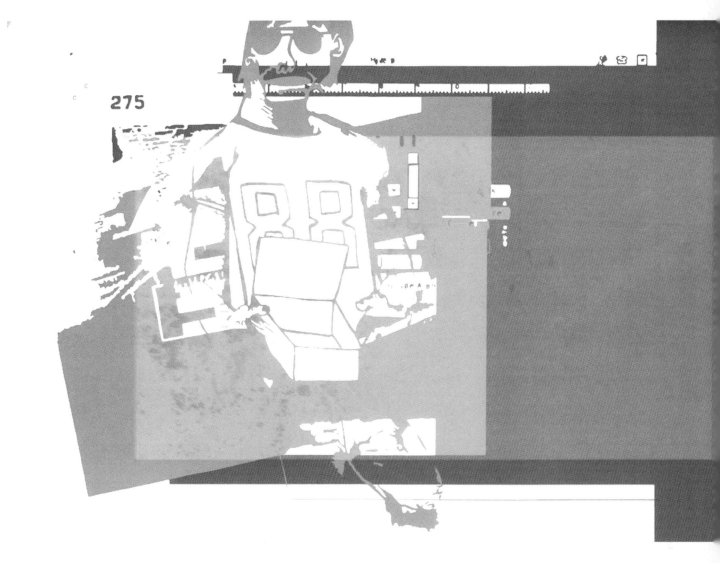

To: 'Karsten Saunte' <ka@...>

From: artefact <artefact@artefact...>

Subject: Re: CV

Cc:

Bcc:

X-Attachments:

>Karsten Saunte, programmer

>... of Science in Electronic ... M.C.S.E.

>Graduated from Technical University of Denmark ... in 1989.

>Main subject: Parallel ... drawing Pipelines (3D Computer graphics)

>Special ... include ... are and ... cal hardware design

... company specialising in tailor made
... software ... hardware design and implementation.
Ranging ... software to financial applications.

>Consultant ... Beyerholm ... communication technology (paging/satellite
Beyerholm ... satellite financial information from Reuters and
... work including ...
Ranging ...

>Chief ... founder of Lunatronic 1997-
... Lunatronic provides ... production and documentation
... ly Departments on Hospitals. The system includes
... the application for teaching and/or guiding of users.

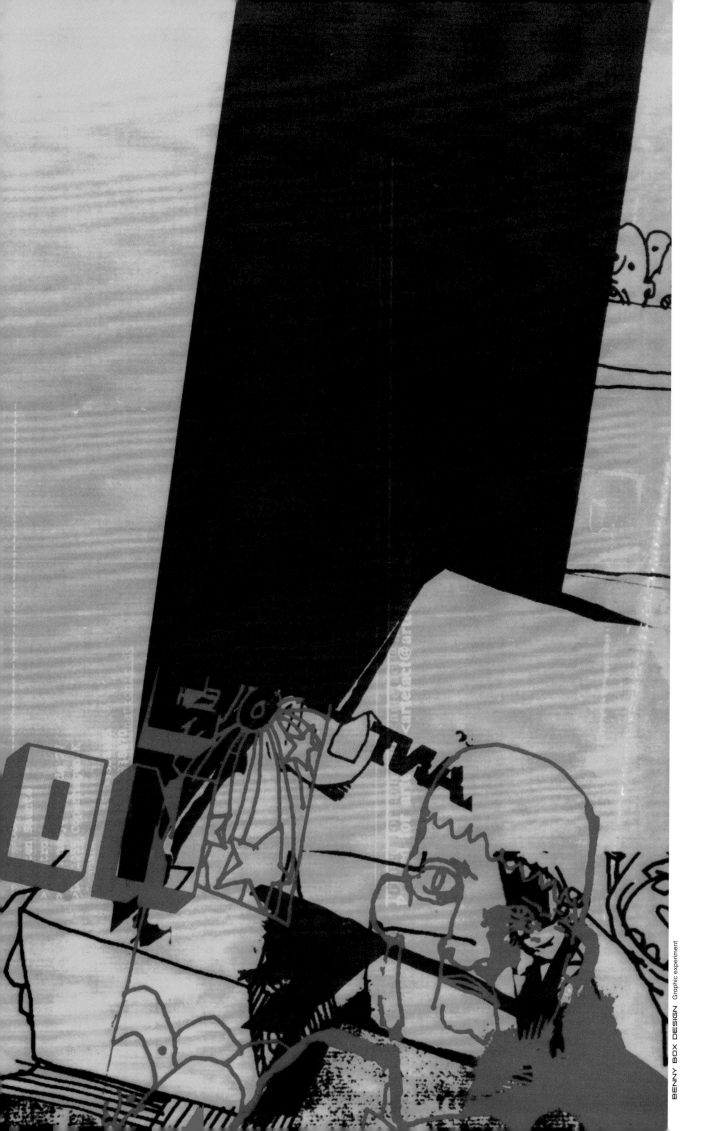

The Shocking Truth!

How it's really like up North. Feature by Thomas Hilland.

SPRENGTE KONA I LUFTA

**NORWEGIAN NEWSPAPER HEADLINE:
'HUSBAND BLEW UP WIFE'**

An old joke: A Swede, a Dane, a Norwegian and a Finn is sitting in a bar. They all raise their glasses and say 'cheers', except the Finn, who asks: 'Are you here to drink or to talk?'

"I'm scared in my own apartment. I'm scared 24 hours a day. But not necessarily in New York. "I actually feel pretty comfortable in New York. I get scared like in Sweden. You know, it's... kind of empty, they're all drunk. Everything works. You know, if you stop at a stop light and don't turn your engine off, people come over and talk to you about it. You go to the medicine cabinet and open it up and there will be a little poster saying: "In case of suicide - call..." You turn on the TV, there's an ear operation. These things scare me. New York? No." Lou Reed in the movie 'Blue in the Face'.

RANET AV JULE- NISSER

ROBBED BY SANTA CLAUSES'

Most Icelanders believe in Elves and Trolls - supernatural beings that stay hidden from view, living in mountains, hills and rocks. There are many examples in Iceland of highway planners being made to re-route roads around supposed elf dwellings. When Iceland's first shopping mall was built, the electrical cables and similar underground installations were laid well away from suspected locations of gnomes and fairies. When planning a new house, people will sometimes hire "elf-spotters" to ensure the site is free of spirit folk.

'If we had dolphins we'd kill them too'. Slogan on best-selling t-shirt in Norway, referring to the foreign criticism of the whale hunt.

Drepte elsker og ektemann med

motorsag og sementblander

'KILLED LOVER AND HUSBAND WITH CHAIN SAW AND CEMENT MIXER'

Three Nordic inventions: Paper clips, dynamite, and soft cheese in a tube.

Denmark is a very flat country. Their highest mountain is called 'Himmelbjerget', which translates as 'The Mountain that reaches into the sky'. It's 147m high.

The Finns and Norwegians are the heaviest coffee drinkers in the world. Elderly and rural people literally force their guests to have some cups, and people with professions that involves visiting homes, like plumbers, have been known to have a high degree of stomach ulcers as a result of this enormous amount of coffee drinking.

VETTSKREMT AV VILL «JESUS»

'TERRIFIED BY CRAZY 'JESUS'

In McDonalds in north Sweden the burgers comes served with knife and fork, as it is the local way to eat them. In Norway you can order a McSalmon. With extra cheese.

The ferry from Norway to Denmark takes twelve hours. The return journey takes only eight. On the outward journey the captain steers the ship around in circles in the middle of international waters to give people the chance to drink as much tax free booze as possible. The next morning though, everyone wants to get home as fast as possible in a straight line, making the journey four hours shorter than the night before.

On the Swedish underground, the signs inform you that the escalators are either going 'Up', or 'Not Up'.

14 RAN MED AGURK

'14 ROBBERIES USING A CUCUMBER'

-You had a visit this Wednesday from President Bongo from Gabon - was he a nice fellow?
-You mean Bongo From Congo? (The Norwegian Foreign Minister trying to be funny on live radio)

«BILRINGEN» VAR EN BABY

'BEER GUT' WAS A BABY'

Beer was prohibited in Iceland for 75 years. In 1989 it finally became legalised, making it possible to have a glass when enjoying Icelandic delicacies such as rams testicles pickled in sour milk, shark meat putrified by being buried in the ground for several months, lambs meat smoked over lamb dung fire, boiled sheep head and the old favourite; soured seal flippers.

In an opinion poll, the Finns were asked the following question: "In your view, how do you think an Estonian would describe a Finn?" The adjectives most often used by the Finns were: rich, friendly, hard-working, helpful, modern, cultivated. Then the Estonians were asked the same question. In their opinion the Finns were: drunk, stupid, mean, indolent, cold, arrogant, reckless. Of course, it *might* have something to do with the Finnish pastime as so called 'vodka-tourists' in Tallinn.

FORFØRT AV MANN I SEXY DAMEUNDERTØY

'SEDUCED BY MAN WEARING SEXY WOMENS UNDERWEAR'

And finally:
A recent American survey has found that blondes really *do* have more fun. It's a scientific fact.

Enjoy the book.

ECLECTIC BOB** Chocolate Garden
Vocals by: Sofia Allard, Daddy Boastin, Scoob Rock, Camela Leierth and Herbie.

PRIMAL MUSIC

ECLECTIC BOB** Chocolate Garden

PRIMCD 006

→ www.eclecticbob.com

PRIMAL MUSIC

Utmärkt Svensk Form 2001   Svensk Form   Stockholm
13 sept – 28 okt   Skeppsholmen   www.svenskform.se

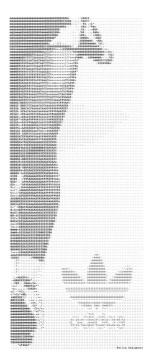

./FILM/

#19

TIM FELDMANN / WILDA

DEREDE
MAND

17–30 maj 2001
mAn––fre KL. 20 + LørDAG kl.16 & 20
Den Anden OPERA, KronPrinsensGADE 7 KBH K.
BiLLetteR 33325556 & BiLLetnEt 70156565
UnGDomSBilleT 45KR. BiLLiGDAG TirsDAG 55 kr.

SPILD AF TID Poster

SPILD AF TID Various animations + stills

leva livet
en film av mikael håfström

kjell bergqvist	carina m johansson	lia boysen	staffan kihlbom
fares fares	josefin peterson	christian fiedler	ulla-britt norrman
eva fritjofson	anders ahlbom rosendahl	bojan westin	eva röse

kostym marie flyckt scenografi gert wibe musik magnus frykberg och kristoffer wallman klippning darek
hodor, sfk foto peter mokrosinski co-producenter peter aalbæk jensen, tomas eskilsson och gunnar carlsson
manus hans gunnarsson och mikael håfström producent anna anthony regi mikael håfström

dts DIGITAL SOUND INDIANA

indiana film i samproduktion med film i väst, trollhättan film ab, svt drama göteborg och med stöd av svenska filminstitutet konsulent niklas rådström, delfinansierat av europeiska regionala utvecklingsfonden distribution sonet film

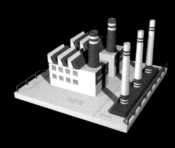 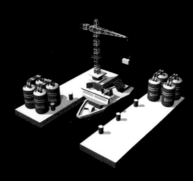 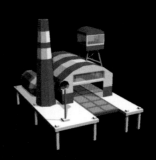

  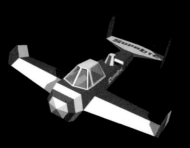

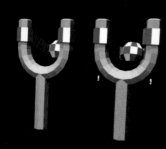  

ACNE Jeans I Netbaby - images

FOR FASHIO

FOR FASHIO

FOR FASHIO

FOR FASHIO

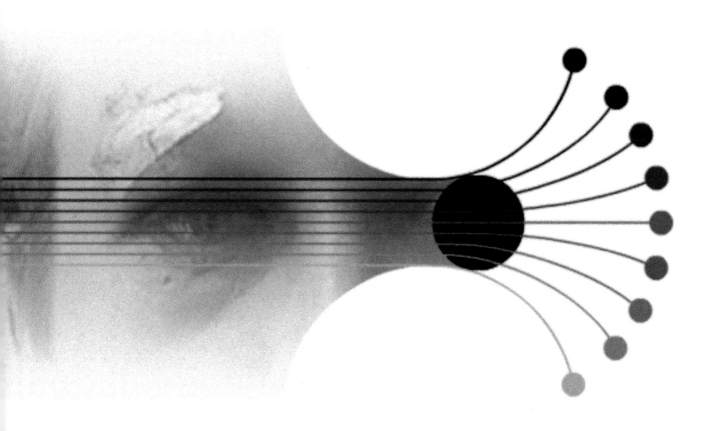

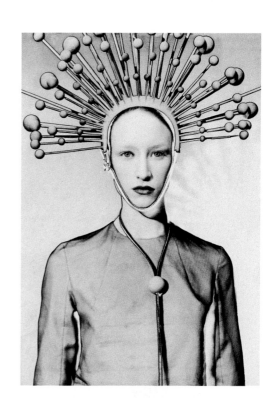

SKÚLI SVERRISSON/HILMAR JENSSON · KJÁR · I. II. III. IV. V. VI. VII. VIII. · SKÚLI SVERRISSON BASSI · HILMAR JENSSON GÍTAR · ALLT EFNI UNNIÐ ÚR SPUNA, · TEKINN UPP Í 4-5. SEPTEMBER 1997
UPPTÖKUSTJÓRN OG ÚRVINNSLA EFNIS: SKÚLI SVERRISSON · STAFRÆN ÚRVINNSLA ÞORSTEINN JÓNSSON · UMSLAGSHÖNNUN & LJÓSM. GOODUR · MYNDSKREYTING Á FRAMHL.: PÉTUR F. BALDVINSSON · ÞAKKIR FÁ ÁSI, VALLA OG TÓTA

HILMAR JENSSON · KERFILL

TRAUST I-V · HILMAR JENSSON, KASSAGÍTAR · KJARTAN VALDEMARSSON, PÍANÓ, KALIMBA · MATTHÍAS M.D. HEMSTOCK, TROMMUR & SLAGVERK · PÉTUR GRÉTARSSON, VÍBRAFÓNN & SLAGVERK · ÖLL TÓNLIST EFTIR FLYTJENDUR
HLJÓÐRITAÐ OG HLJÓÐBLANDAÐ Í HLJÓÐVERI FÍH 8-9 JÚLÍ 1998 · UPPTÖKUMAÐUR: ÍVAR BONGÓ · STAFRÆN ÚTFÆRSLA: ÍVAR BONGÓ
UMSLAGSHÖNNUN OG LJÓSMYNDUN: GOODUR · MYNDSKREYTING Á FRAMHLIÐ: PÉTUR F. BALDVINSSON · ÞAKKIR FÁ ANDRÉS Í TÓNASTÖÐINNI OG ÁSI.

KERFILL · #011 · HILMAR JENSSON · GÍTAR · ANDREW D'ANGELO·ALTÓSAXÓFÓNN OG BASSAKLARÍNETT · ÓSKAR GUÐJÓNSSON·TENÓR OG SÓPRANSAXÓFÓNN · EYÞÓR GUNNARSSON· PÍANÓ · BRYNDÍS HALLA GYLFADÓTTIR· SELLÓ · MATTHÍAS M.D. HEMSTOCK·TROMMUR OG SLAGVERK
TÓNLIST EFTIR HILMAR JENSSON · HLJÓÐRITAÐ Í HLJÓÐVERI FÍH 19. OG 20. JANÚAR 1999 · UPPTÖKUMAÐUR ÍVAR RAGNARSSON · HLJÓÐBLANDAÐ Í STÚDÍÓ SEPTEMBER 17. OG 18. ÁGÚST · UMSJÓN UMSLAGS OG LJÓSMYNDUN ·GOODUR· · MYNDSKREYTING Á FRAMHLIÐ· PÉTUR F. BALDVINSSON ·
ÞAKKIR FÁ FLYTJENDUR, ÁSI, ÍVAR OG MENNINGARSJÓÐUR FÍH

VS. PAUL LYDON
KITCHEN MOTORS · MYRKRAVERK
VESTURPORTIÐ
LAUGARDAGINN 9. MARS 2002
KL. 22.00 - 500KALL

If you will come up next week we will finish that portrait.

FOR ONCE
I WOULD LIKE TO DO THIS RIGHT

PROGRESS

this is my space

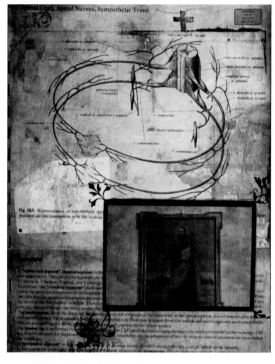

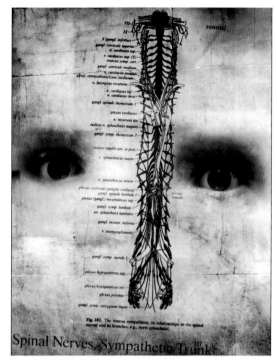

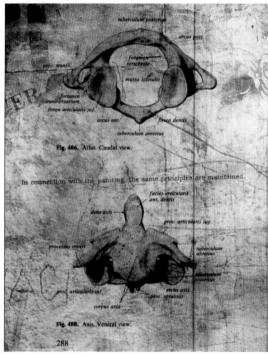

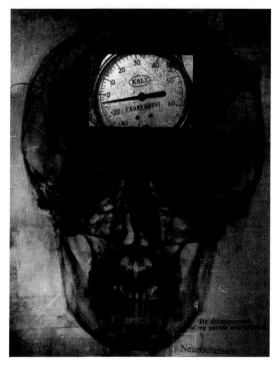

UNITED DRAMA AIRLINES ACTING PRESENTS ::
drama
Leikstjórn: Jóhann Halldórsson
AÐALHLUTVERK: Gabríel Kristjánsson, Finnur Eyjólfsson, Margrét Harðardóttir, Eygló Finnsdóttir, Þorsteinn Guðmundsson, Þorgerður Gunnarsdóttir
ÞÝÐING: Hafliði Höskuldsson Sýnt hjá Leikfélagi Menntaskólans á Akureyri
Consetetur sadipscing elitr, sed diam nonumy eirmod tempor invidunt ut labore et dolore magna aliquyam erat, sed diam voluptua. At vero eos et accusam et justo duo dolores et ea rebum. Stet clita kasd gubergren, no sea takimata sanctus est Lorem ipsum dolor sit amet. Lorem ipsum dolor sit amet, consetetur sadipscing elitr, sed diam nonumy eirmod tempor invidunt ut labore et dolore magna aliquyam erat, sed diam voluptua. At vero eos et accusam et justo duo dolores et ea rebum. Stet clita kasd gubergren, no sea

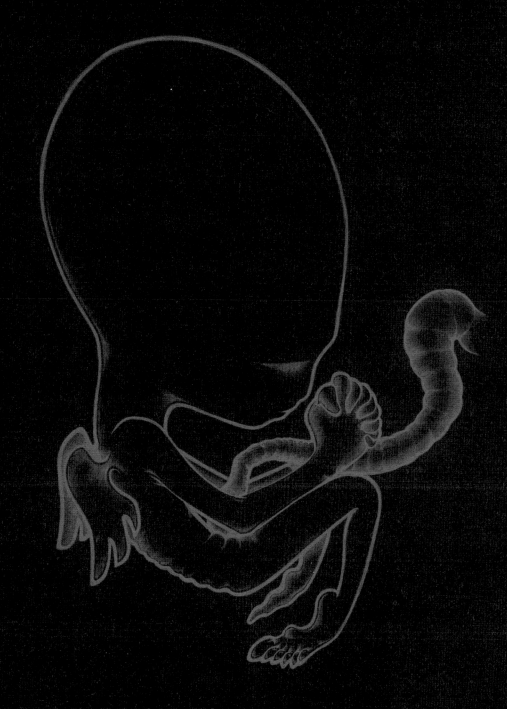

ÁGUST REYÐAR GUNNARSSON

motor.ax
-barry adamson
+pan sonic

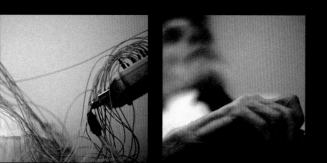

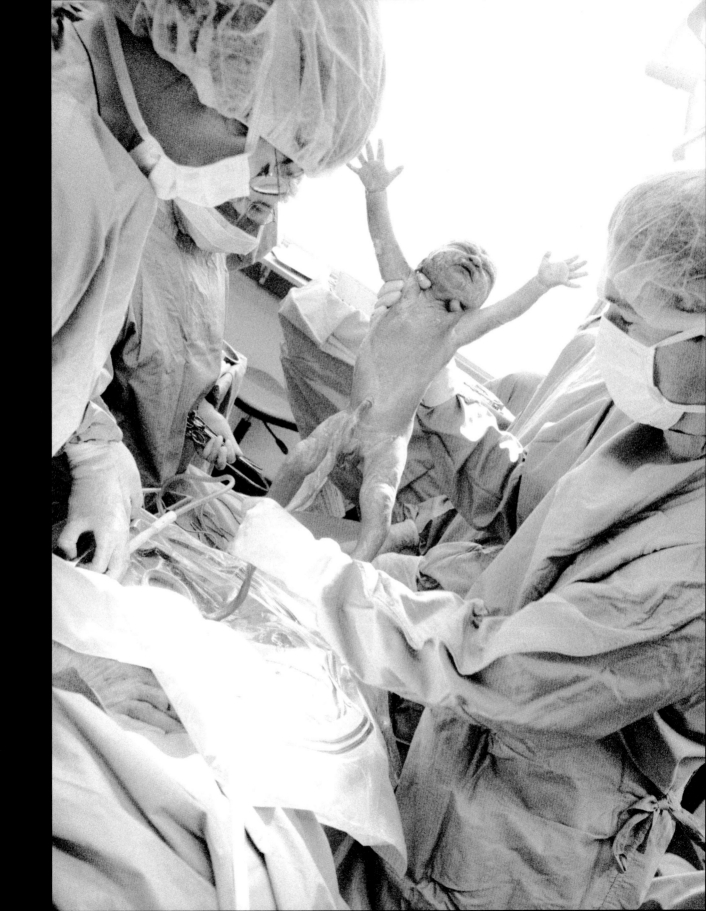

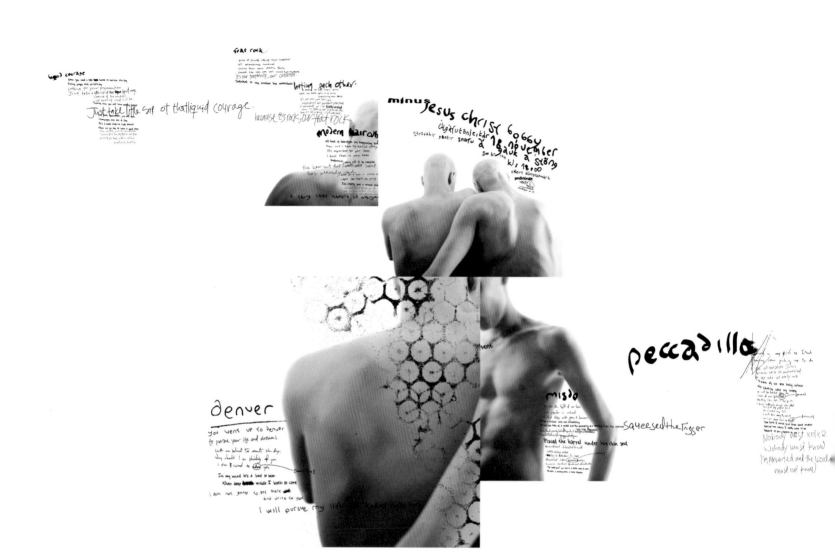

chimera
leisure
modern haircuts
misjo
electra complex
denver
frat rock
arctic exhibition
liquid courage
peccadillo
pulse

jesus christ bobby

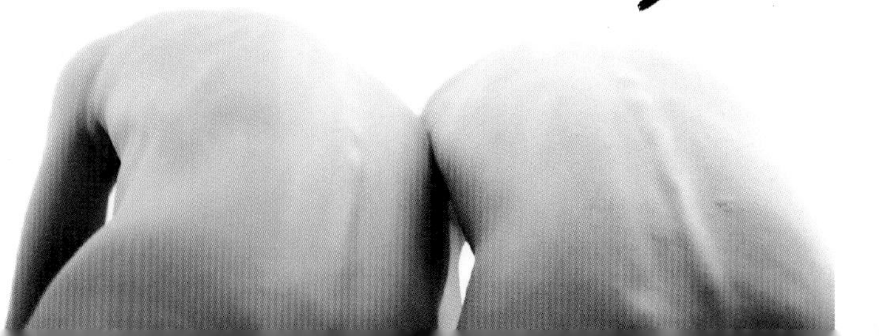

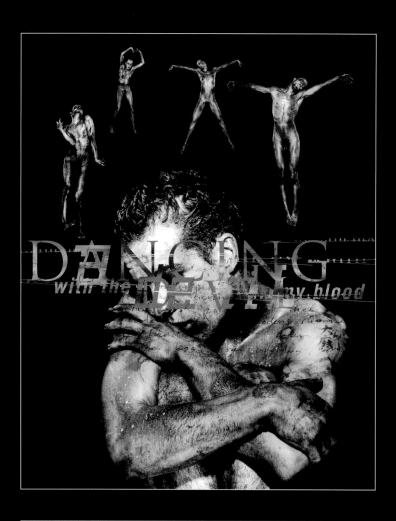

EKHORNFORSS / NON-FORMAT Interview

Is there something you really love or hate about Scandinavia in general? Being based in London it is easy to see the positive side of the Norwegian climate, the raw nature, the snowy winters, the surplus of woods, mountains and space.

Is there something like a Scandinavian identity in graphic design and if so, what makes it Scandinavian? I have always looked at graphic design as an international discipline where cultural differences make for variations rather than distinct identities. I think Norwegian design in general has taken it's main inspiration from Swiss modernism and adapted it into a pragmatic but slick aesthetic that emphasizes prettiness and 'correctness' rather than raw energy and brutality.

This is a very broad generalization but this impression was cemented by comparing the higher graphic design education in Norway to the UK. Of course there are good designers in Norway who look at what is going on elsewhere and take inspiration from it. I guess this book will be more inclined to celebrate those designers rather than the traditionalists.

Is there a Scandinavian design community outside of Scandinavia? Or does it all mix up? I don't feel we belong to a Scandinavian design community as such. We identify and communicate with designers from the rest of the world as much as those from Scandinavia but it has been exciting to see a few excellent Norwegian designers and photographers coming through during the late nineties. Kim Hiorthøy and Sølve Sundsbø are two we have found particularly inspiring.

Scandinavian people seem to care about hipness, are hypes important as an engine for change? Trends, fashion, hype etc are definitely a great driving force for change. It keeps the visual language fresh. A universal aesthetic that is attractive to everyone, regardless of when a piece of design is produced, has yet to be found. Let's hope nobody does.

How did the web influence you? The web was always bound to circulate ideas at an unprecedented rate and without the normal hierarchies of the establishment. It is certainly one of the things that blurs the distinctions between one nation's design characteristics and another. Up until very recently design books were the only means of information on what another nation's designers were up to. Today you can roam the net and take pleasure in discovering them for yourself. It's a field day for original designers and copycats alike.

At Non-Format we actively use the web. For example, it has become our main source for finding new and interesting type designers. It has also increased the speed of the design process. We can now jpeg visuals over to the client, receive feedback and send a job off to print without having a traditional meeting. This is both positive and negative

I guess, but why dwell on the negative aspects when there is so much that is positive. The feeling here is that the influence of the web has only just begun.

Scandinavian designers are working all over the world in important companies and on their own. Do they bring a Scandinavian touch to these projects? And do they take international experiences back to Scandinavia? I'm very seldom taken for an Englishman so I guess I still display my origins. Growing up with a different set of cultural icons, children's stories, TV shows etc. brings up different angles and points of view in the creative process which is both refreshing and useful.

Is there a special social/political approach? There is a strong sense of political correctness in Norway so I imagine it comes across in the design as well but I can't say I'm familiar enough to give any examples.

Is Scandinavian design sexy? Good design is sexy. Brilliant ideas are very sexy!

What sets your personal work apart from your commercial projects? At the moment it all blends together. We are lucky enough to have many clients demanding creative work in which we can voice our personal visual preoccupations. We don't therefore have a massive surplus of personal work that we are waiting to be able to use.

Is the balance between aesthetics and message in design handled differently by Scandinavian designers? Not sure.

What would you do if graphic design didn't exist? I would invent it, bring hierarchy to the flow of information, become rich and famous and live happily ever after.

Do you miss the landscapes/dark winters/midsummer nights and does that influence your design? When London is misty and grey I miss it all! I always loved the climate of the arctic but the fact that I have spent the last nine years here tells its own story. I'm no longer sure if home sickness and melancholy play a big part in my design process but I like to think those long arctic winters are still with me.

What influence does traditional folkloristic art and pop art have on your work? Pop art was one of the main inspirations for going into graphics in the first place. Part of Andy Warhol's Pop art pointed directly to graphic design, claiming that a piece of packaging could be a piece of art in its own right. This was a great eye opener for someone who was never particularly turned on by traditional painting or folklore art. We still look to art for inspiration and sometimes have 'arty' ideas for projects but we don't confuse what we are doing with fine art. We'll go down any avenue that seems interesting and exciting but at the end of the day we are just helping to fill the market with mass produced objects for people to love, hate or feel indifferent to.

What would you do if you were not a designer? Sell our Letraset collection.

MONDAY BAR Techno Experience///

EKHORNFORSS/NON-FORMAT CD covers

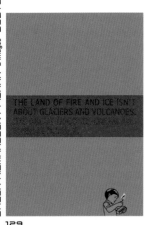

JASSA PALMARSSON / PSAKK 2 images SUBTOPIA CD cover ZURGLUB image

THIS POSTER ANNOUNCES A NEW BAND WITH A NEW SOUND:

HATTLER

NO EATS YES – TOUR | **THE BAND IS:**

SANDIE WOLLASCH – VOCALS | **NKECHI MBAKWE – VOCALS**

SEBASTIAN STUDNITZKY – TRUMPET | **OLI RUBOW – DRUMS**

HELLMUT HATTLER – BASS

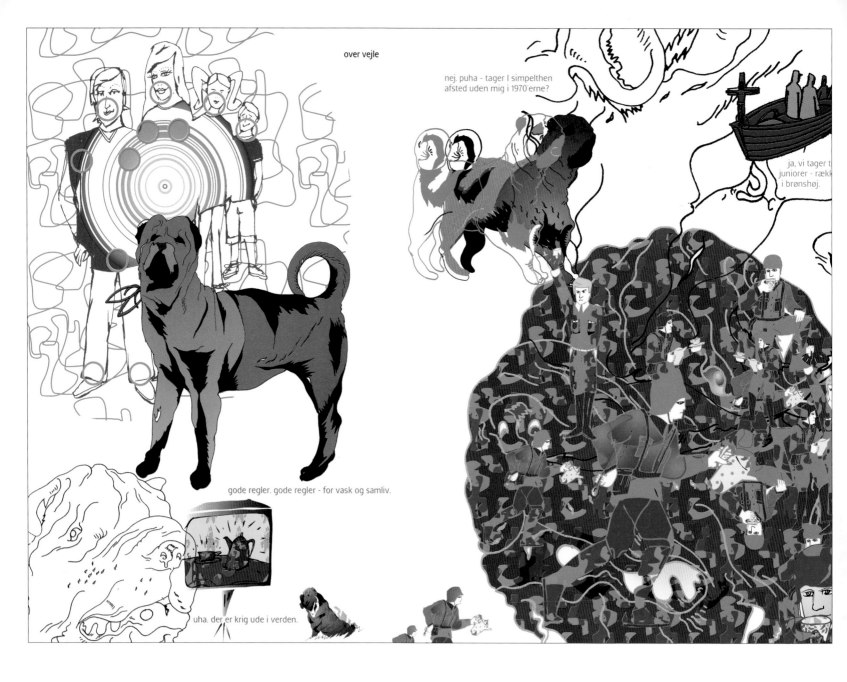

over vejle

nej. puha - tager I simpelthen
afsted uden mig i 1970'erne?

ja, vi tager t
juniorer - rækk
i brønshøj.

gode regler. gode regler - for vask og samliv.

uha. der er krig ude i verden.

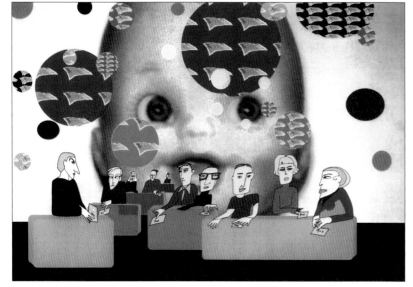

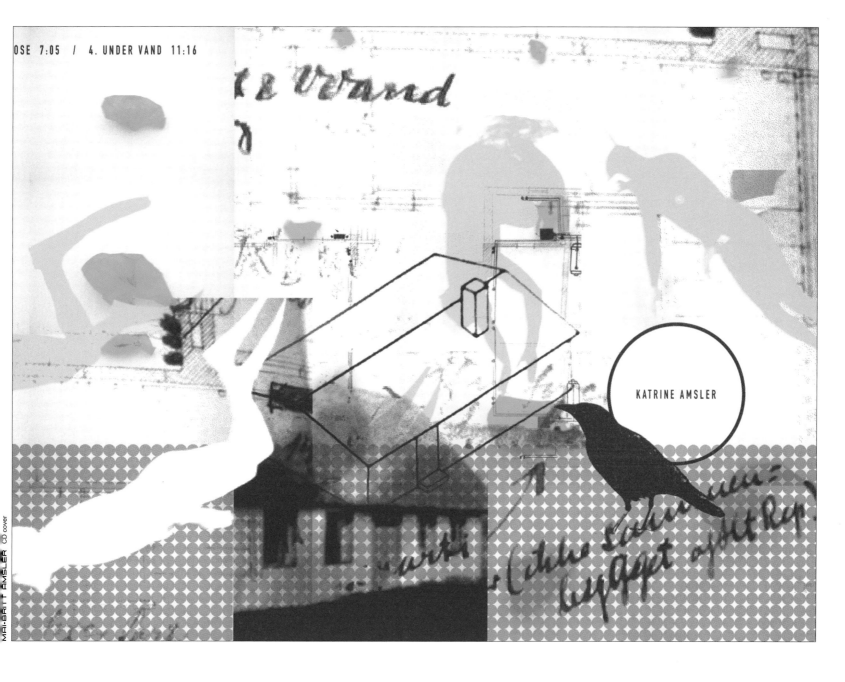

OSE 7:05 / 4. UNDER VAND 11:16

KATRINE AMSLER

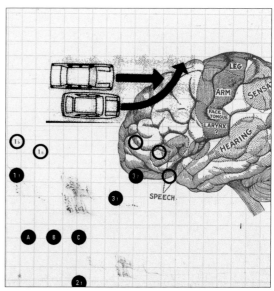

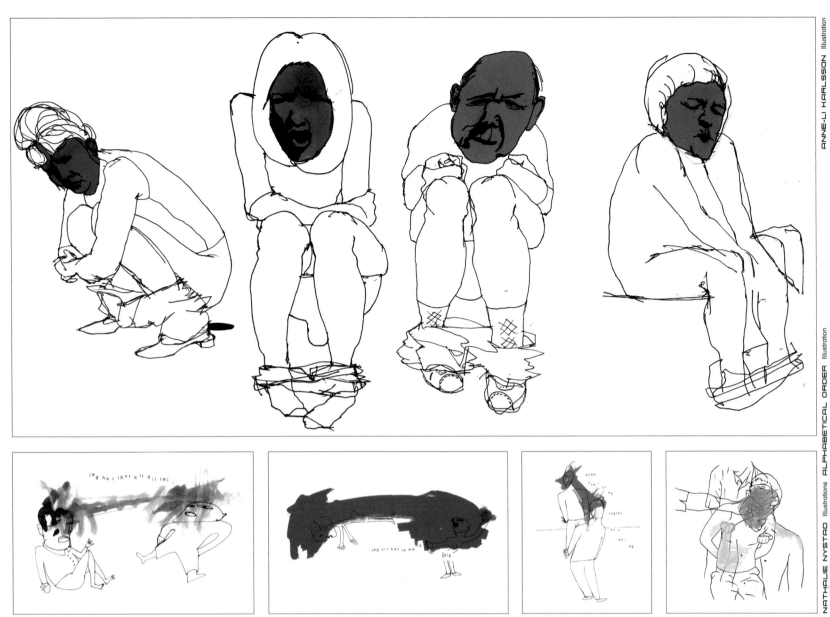

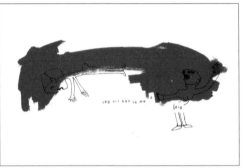

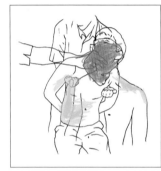

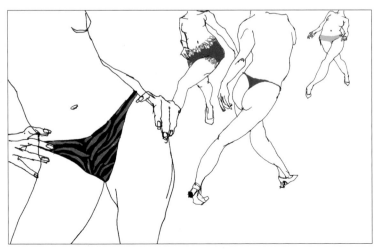
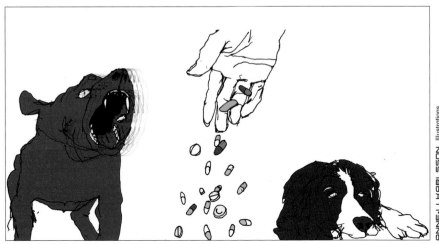

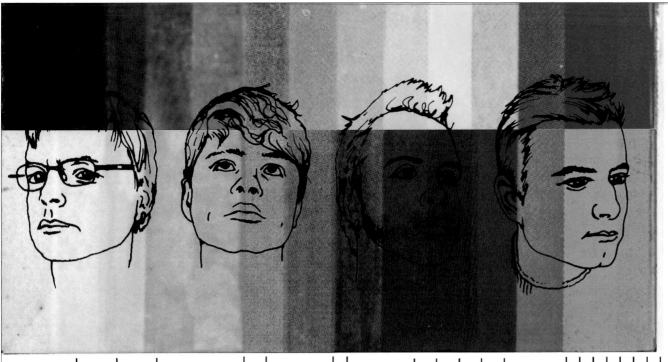

QUANTUM RIDER

LARRY AND THE LEFTHANDED

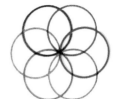

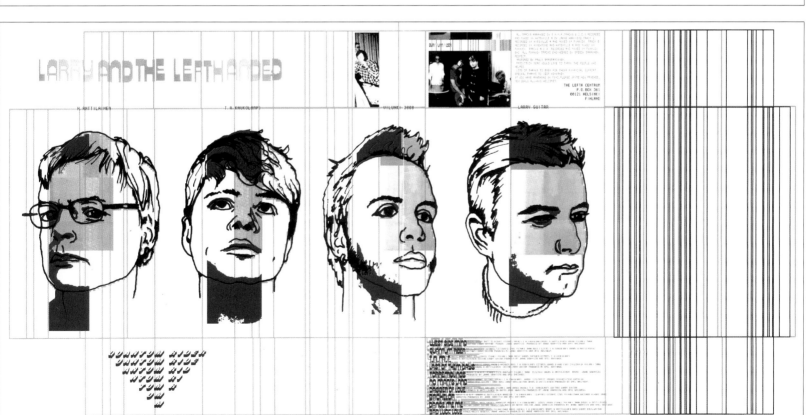

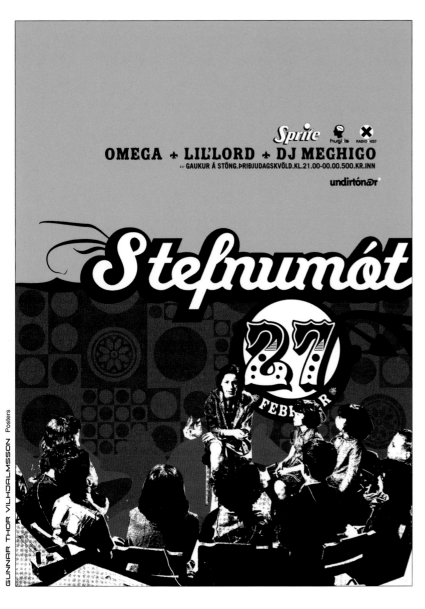

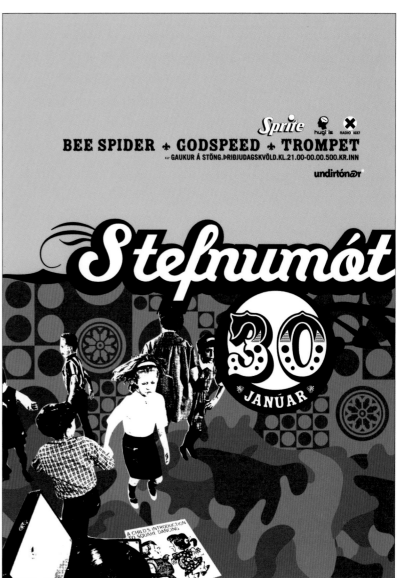

GUNNAR THOR VILHJALMSSON 1, Poster JOHN J. CANDY DESIGN 2, Poster | 4, Illustration KINGSIZE 3, Poster GUNNAR THOR VILHJALMSSON Posters

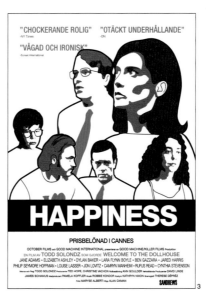

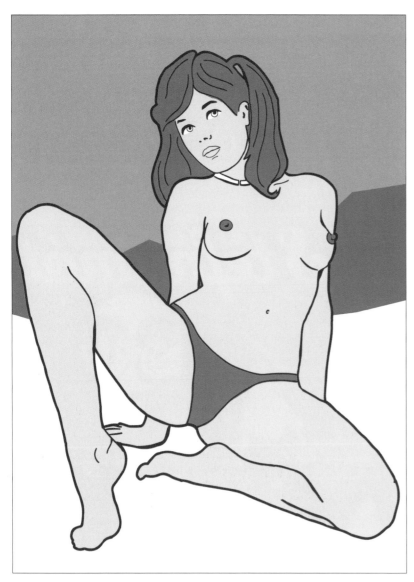

FRANS CARLQVIST Illustrations

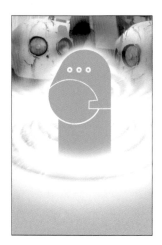

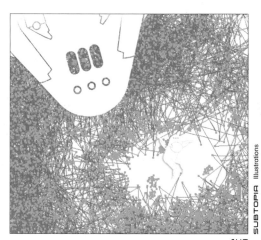

SUBTOPIA Illustrations

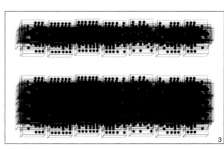

WET PAINT

LAWRENCE LAMB / STEPHEN BAILEY / NEIL HARRIS / KRISTIAN LABAK / TOM DEE / MIRIAM TORRELL / LEE / SIMON SCOTT / LLEWELLYN ROBINSON / MANISHA PANKHANIA / A2

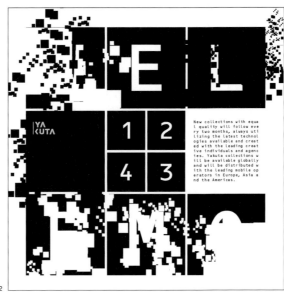

WELCOME
YAKUTA
1 2 3 4

New collections with equal quality will follow every two months, always utilizing the latest technologies available and created with the leading creative individuals and agencies. Yakuta collections will be available globally and will be distributed with the leading mobile operators in Europe, Asia and the Americas.

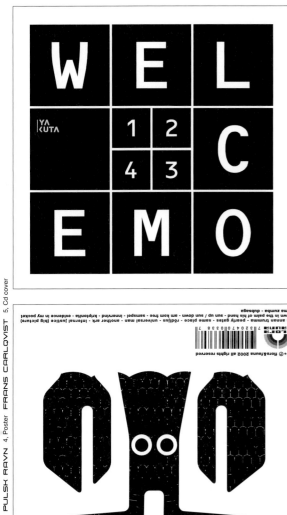

en annan trumma - pearly gates - same place - rådlus - universal man - another ark - internal justice [big picture] - down in the palm of his hand - sun up / sun down - am kom tre - samspel - innervind - kryptonita - evidence in my pocket - toma zumba - dubsaga

moder jords massiva - ur djupen

moder jords massiva - ur djupen / toma zumba - dubsaga / en annan trumma - pearly gates - same place - rådlus / innervind - universal man - another ark - internal justice [big picture] - down in the palm of his hand - sun up / sun down - am kom tre - samspel - reldem - kryptonita - evidence in my pocket

BEAUTIFUL BREAKDOWN

DANCE ENSEMBLE
URBAN ELVES

13–21 SEPTEMBER
MANDAG–LØRDAG KL.20.00
DANSESCENEN ØSTER FÆLLED TORV 34 KØBENHAVN Ø
BILLETTER: 3543 2021 ELLER BILLETNET: 7015 6565

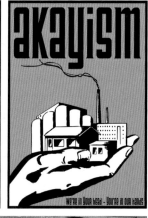

HHIV Akayism I éxcept 1,2,3 FINN HHLLIN

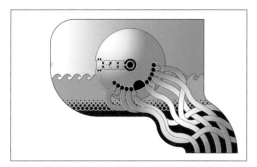

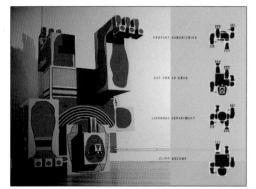

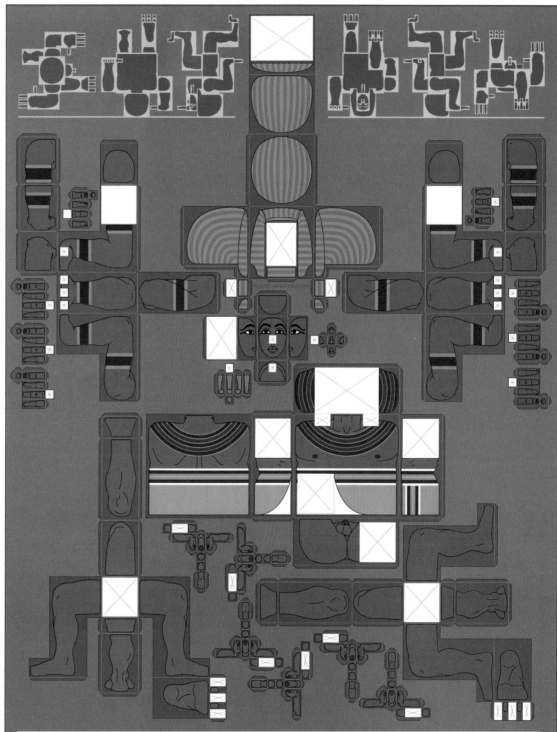

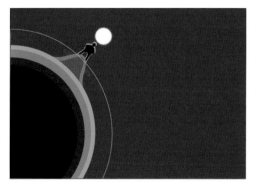

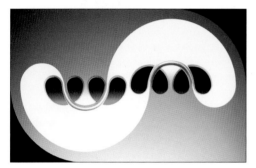

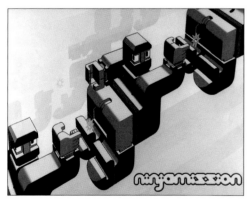

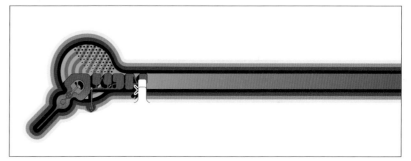

design design
design design design design design design design design design design design design design design design design design design design design
design design
design design design design design design design design design design design design design design design design design design design

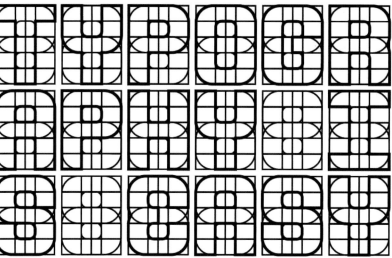

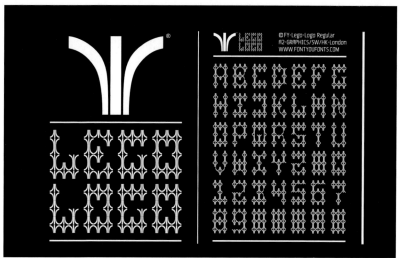

©FY-Lego-Logo Regular
A2-GRAPHICS/SW/HK-London
WWW.FONTYOUFONTS.COM

MONGREL · Pattern · Wallpaper SYRUP HELSINKI Pattern

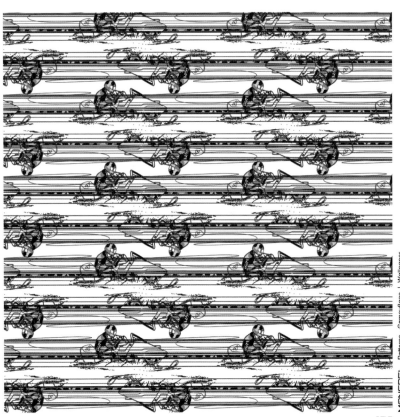

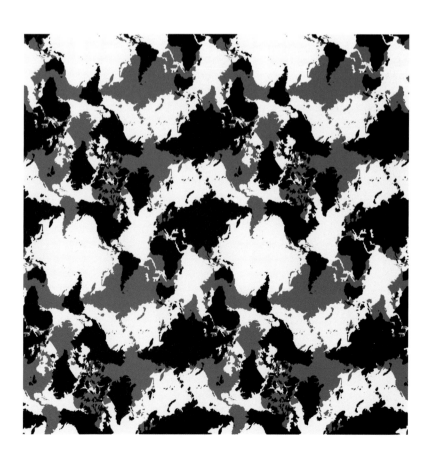

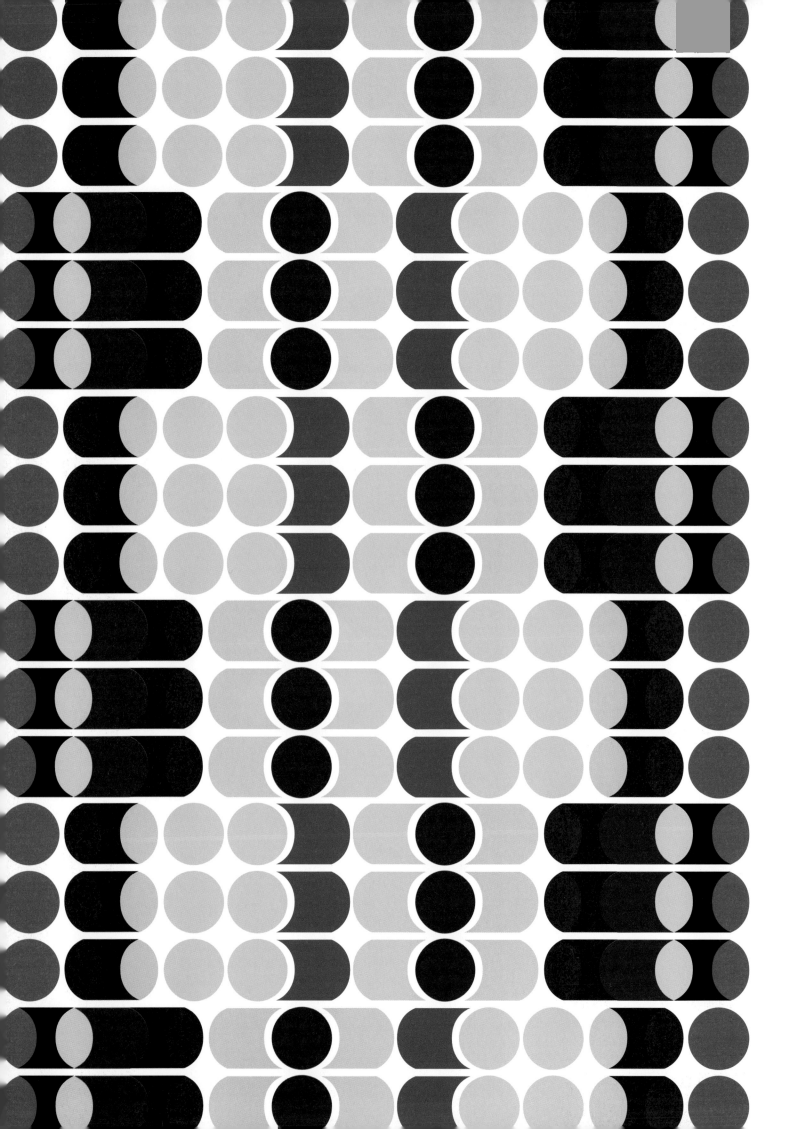

LOTTA KÜHLHORN »The Party«

SPUNK

KIM HIORTHØY Record sleeve

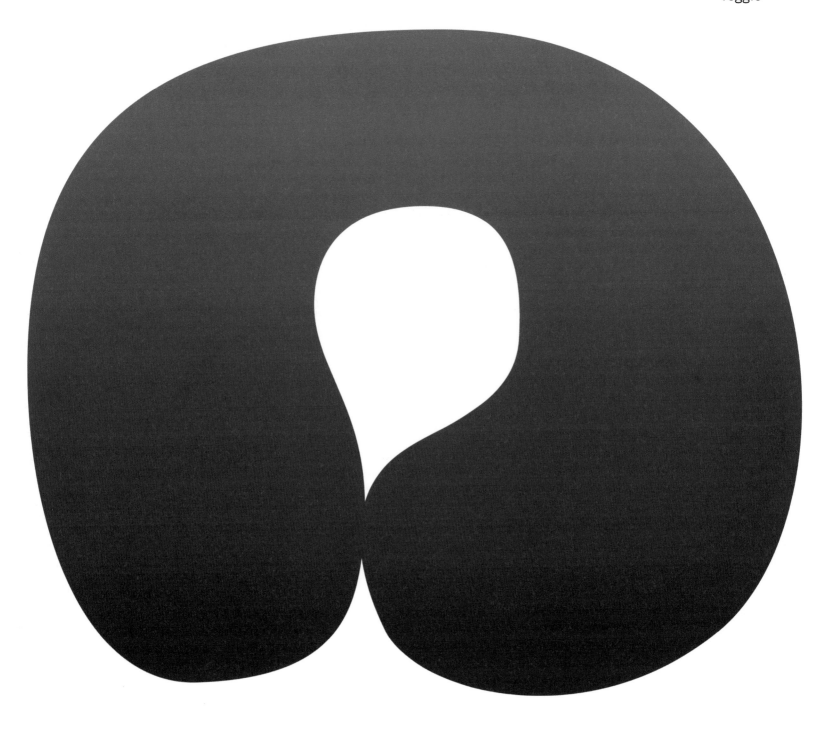

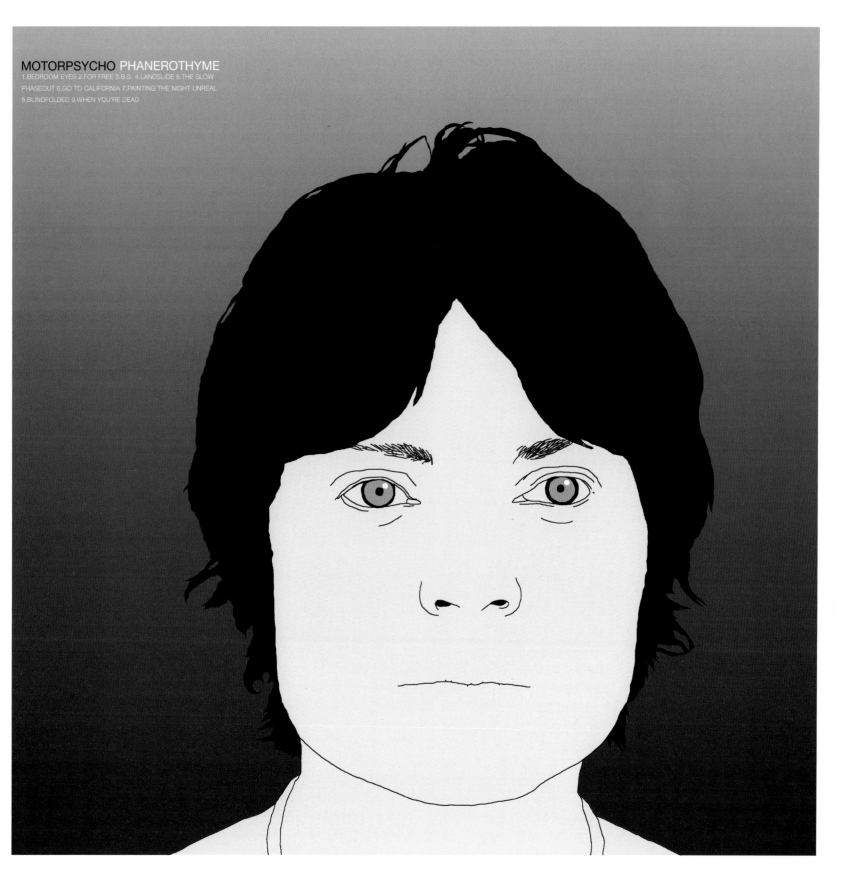

tore elgarøy
the sound of the sun

kim hiorthøy "Hei" 13.10.00 smalltown supersound
www.smalltownsupersound.com

luigi archetti / bo wiget
low tide digitals

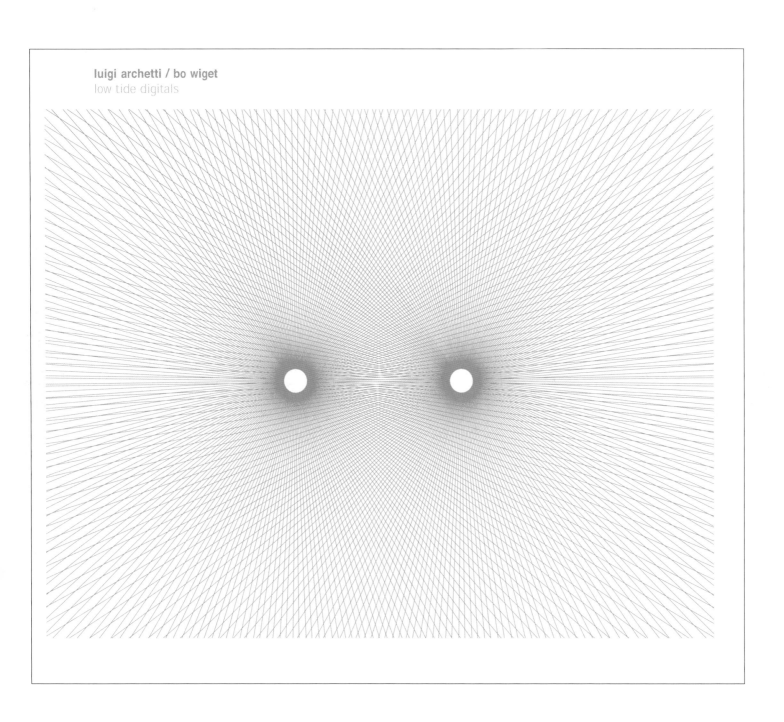

2GD/2GRAPHICDESIGN

KIM HIORTHØY Illustration

monolight
free music

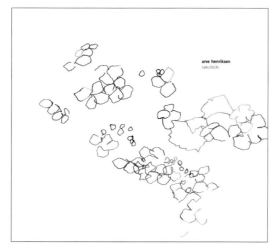

arve henriksen
sakuteiki

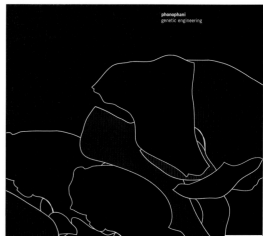

phonophani
genetic engineering

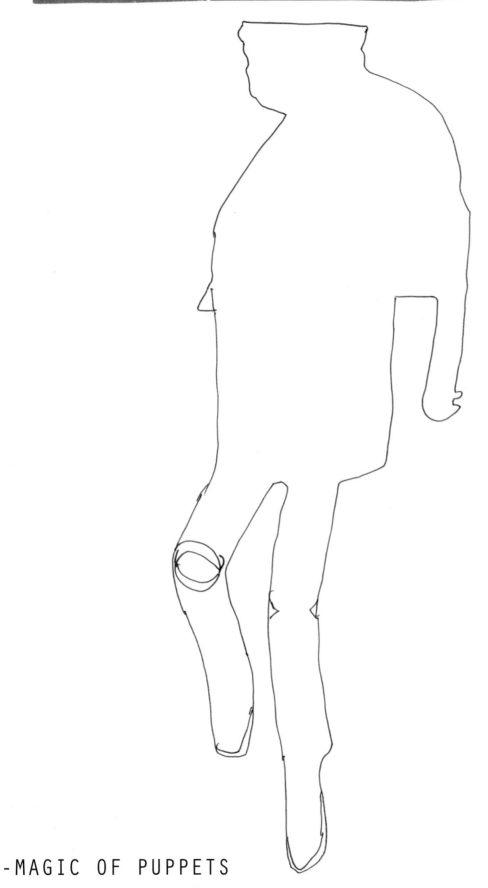

Hvad du ønsker skal du få

-MAGIC OF PUPPETS

-INTERNATIONAL DUKKE- OG FIGURFESTIVAL
-HOEJE TAASTRUPS KOMMUNES BIBLIOTEKER
-29 SEPTEMBER - 6 OKTOBER 2000

ELIN KJØSNES / STAVANGERILLUSTRATØRENE »Summer« I »Rabitt and Cowboy«

BENNY BOX DESIGN Illustration

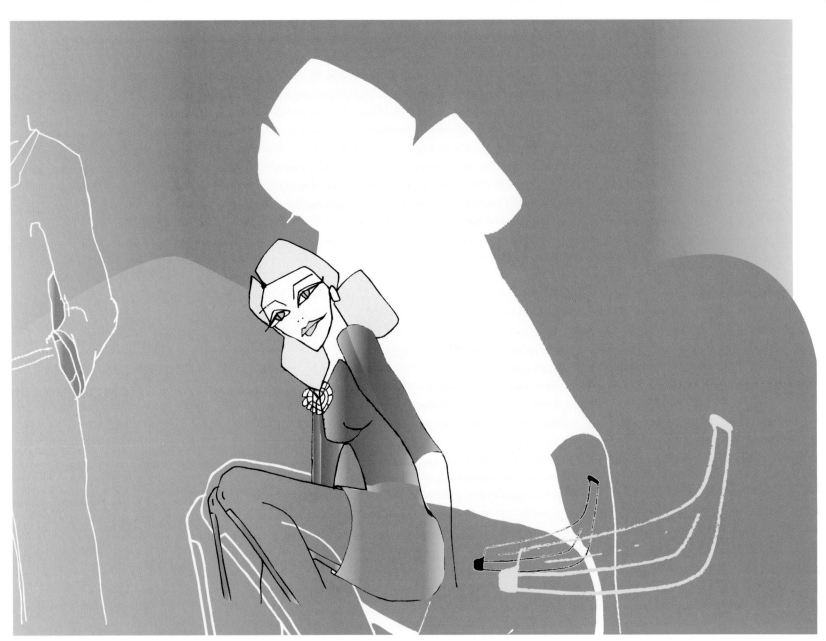

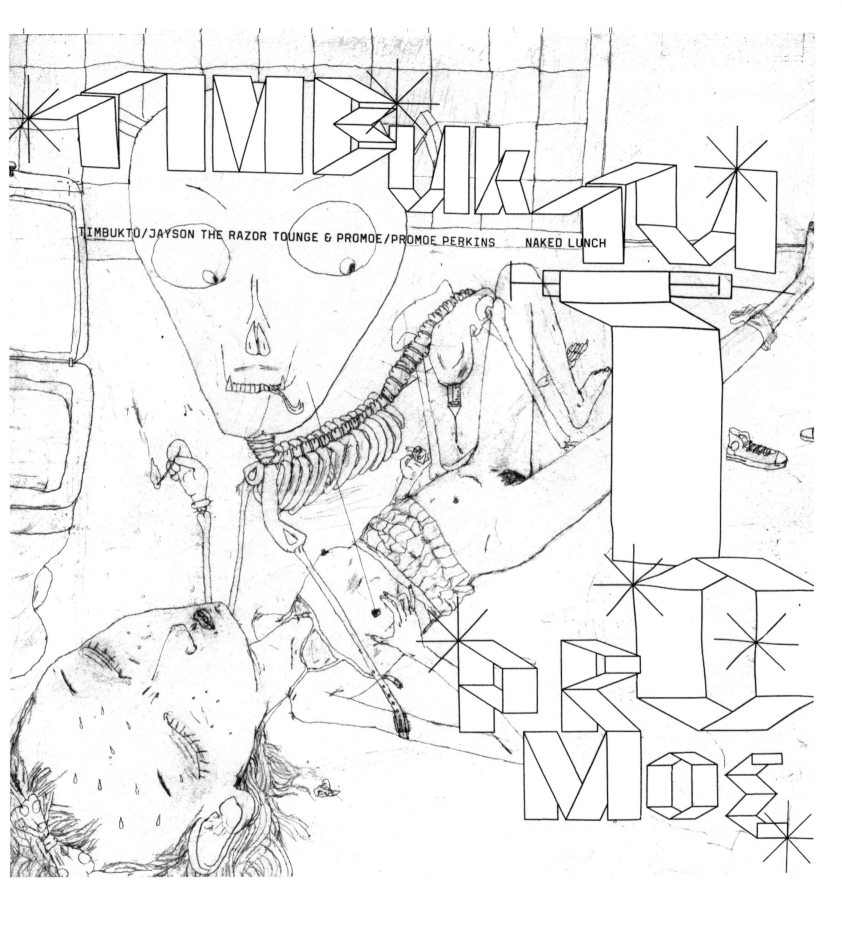

TIMBUKTU/JAYSON THE RAZOR TOUNGE & PROMOE/PROMOE PERKINS   NAKED LUNCH

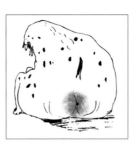

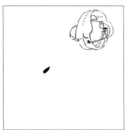

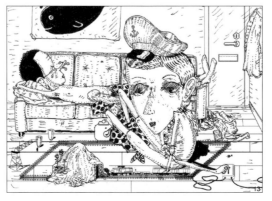

NINA BEIER 1,10 OSKAR KORSAR 12,13,14 NATHALIE NYSTAD 6,7,8,9 ANNE-LI KARLSSON 3,4,5,11 PIKE 2

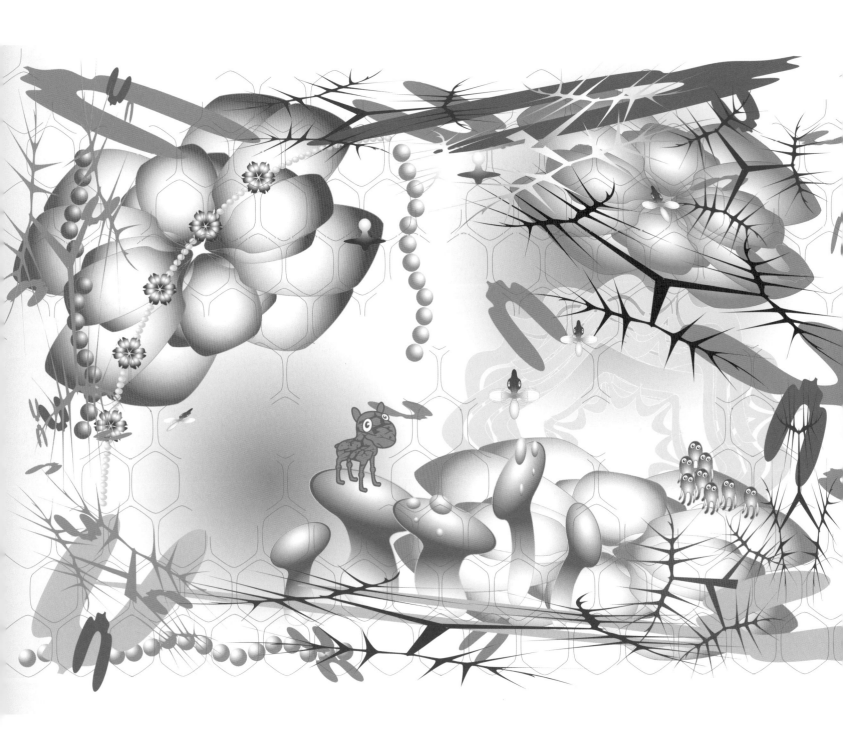

TORSTEN HØGH RASMUSSEN / GULSTUE Movie stills

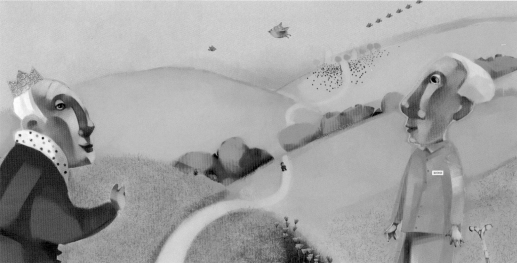

s*k*f*
Söngkeppni
framhaldsskólanema

28. apríl 2001, kl. 14:00,
Háskólabíó (sal 1).

25 skólar taka þátt
Miðaverð er 1200 kr.

FÉLAG FRAMHALDSSKÓLANEMA

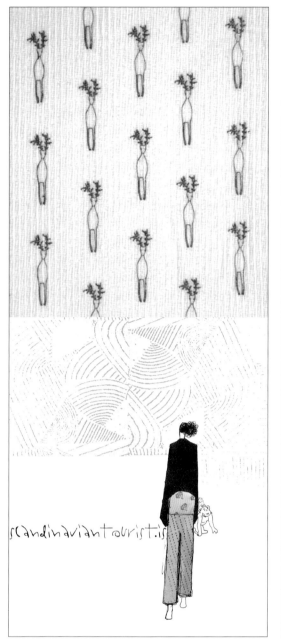

sekterisk lína
scandinavian tourist

scandinaviantourist.is

design house

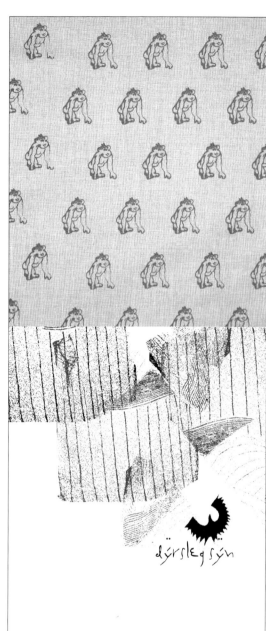

dýrsleg sýn

THE STORY OF
unnur ros

Kíkt í skissubækur

She didn't like it, but I liked it myself.
Like, Nicole, Frauke, Koos
Communication Art & Design, Royal College of Art
Woshow Gallery, Simeon Gregory Street 13-22 (15)
6th March-11th March, 12-22 (15)
Private view 7th March 18-21

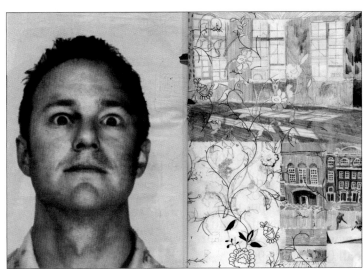

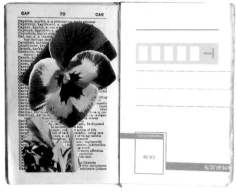

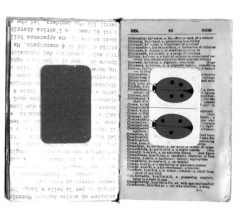

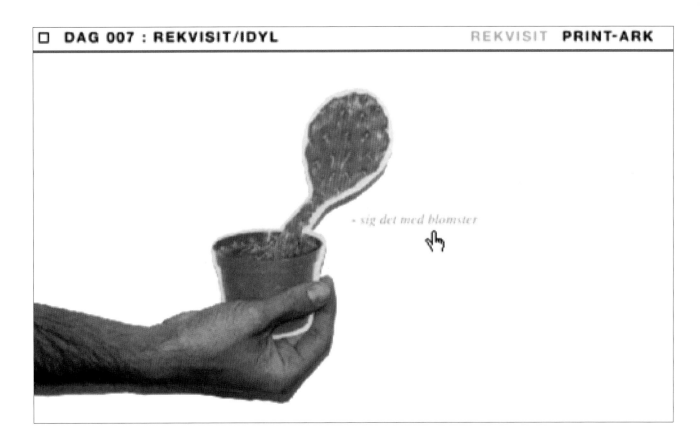

- sig det med blomster

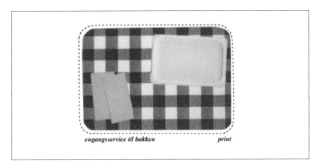

engangsservice til bakken   *print*

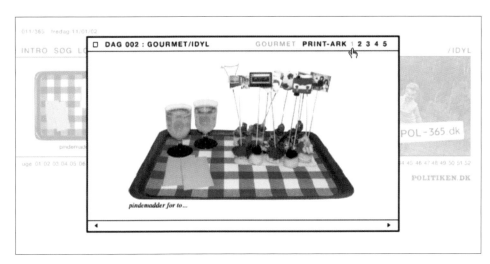

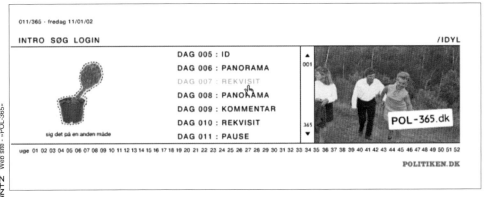

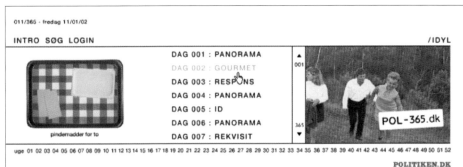

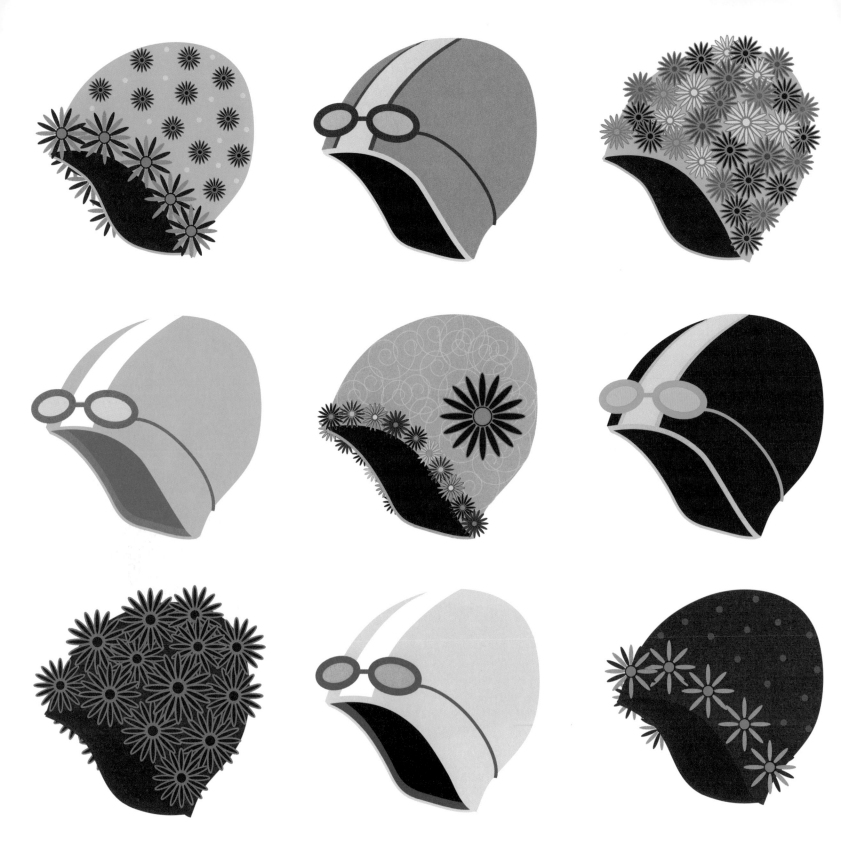

mountain

PIA WALL / STAVANGERILLUSTRATØRENE Illustration · Pin up book / chapter divider

PIA WALL / STAVANGERILLUSTRATØRENE Illustration - Pin up book / chapter divider

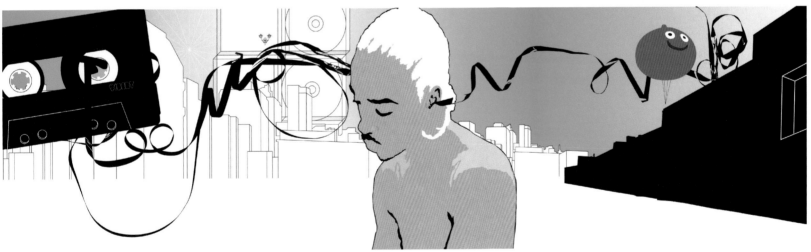

KRISTOFER ÅSTRÖM & HIDDEN TRUCK
CONNECTED

KRISTOFER ÅSTRÖM & HIDDEN TRUCK
NORTHERN BLUES

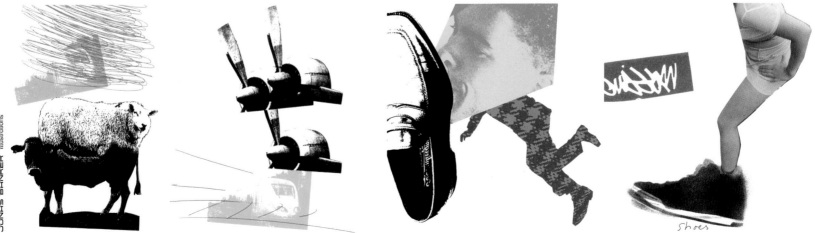

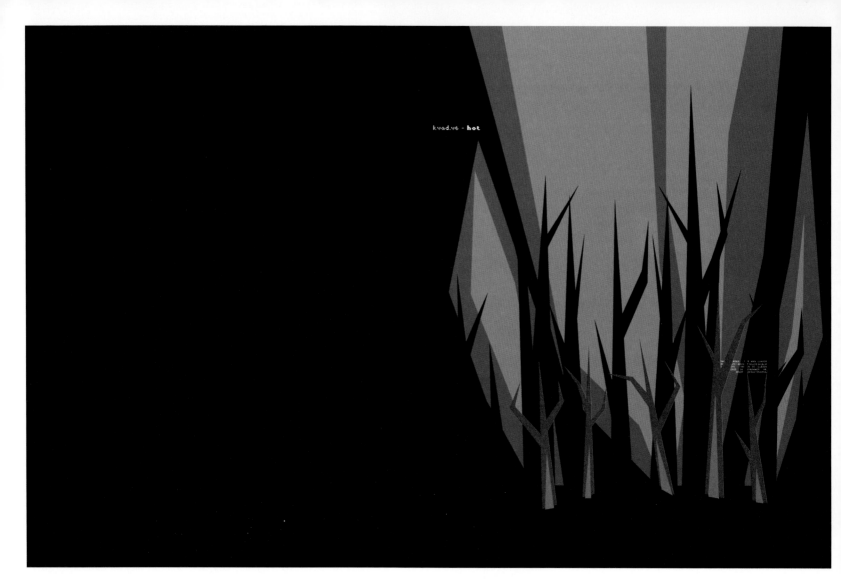

kvad.v6 - **hot**

LERA space bike

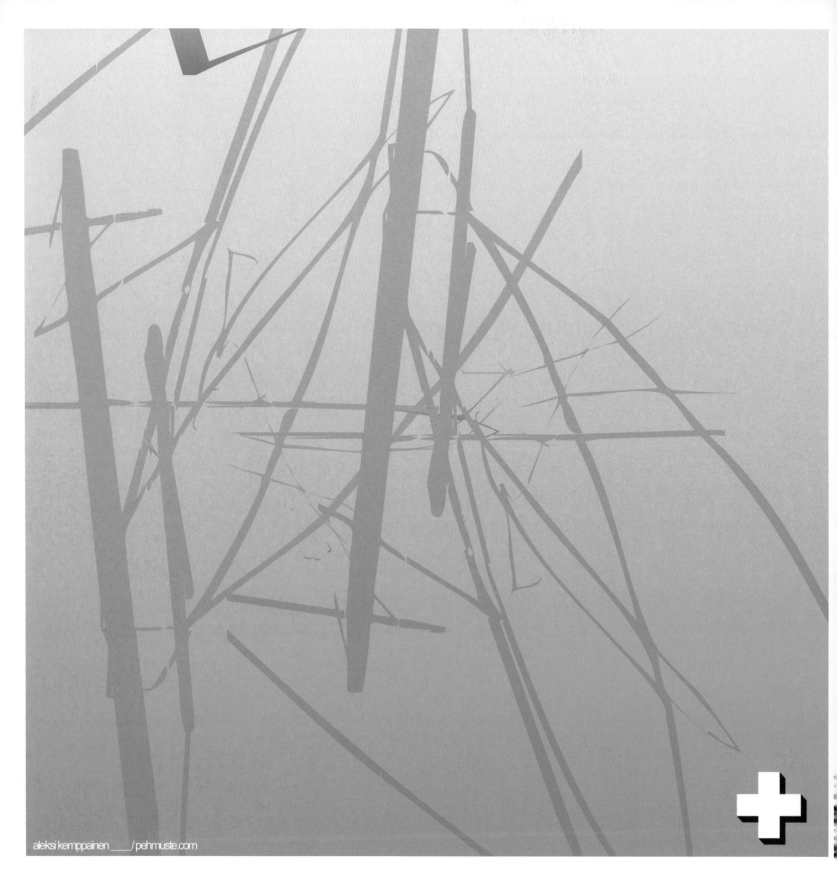

aleksi kemppainen ____/pehmuste.com

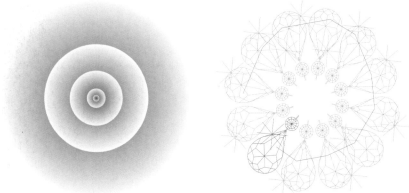

INNERspace

earth+

neue mars

kvad.v6

europa minor

innerspace destinations

SAILING ALONG THROUGH LIFE GAZING AT THE STARS HOPING FOR SOMETHING ELSE **KVAD.V6**
2001 IE4+ NSCAPE4+ JSCRIPT DHTML ETC

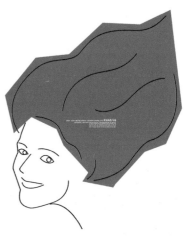

VÅR Wallpaper

24HR INTERNATIONAL AB

Ricky Tillblad
artworks on page: 014 CD cover, 015 image, 022 Magazine cover, 050/051 Logo, 098 Poster
home country: Sweden • living/working in Stockholm, Sweden
fax: +46 8 442 97 79 • email: ricky@24hr.se • url: www.24hr.se
date of birth / date of foundation: 04/12/67 / 01/09/99
CV / short company history/ studies/ education: Studies at "Grafiska Tecknare" in Lund/ Sweden. Started design company "F+" 1988. Started "24HR" in 1999.
latest personal / commercial projects: Baxter Web / www.baxtered.com
Do the landscapes/dark winters/midsummer nights have an effect on your soul and design? Yes. What influence have traditional folkloristic art and pop art on your work? Not much I think. But I like Anders Zorns paintings. What would you do if you were not a designer? A Gardener. Do you feel, there is a Scandinavian (design) identity or special approach? I guess it would be the blond clean style. What are your inspirations, aims, dreams and what's your philosophy? Inspirated by my dreams. Philosophy; "if you should do it, do it the best way - or don't".

2GD

Jan Nielsen / Ole Lund
artworks on page: 100 Catalogue, 113 Catalogue image, 163 Card, 210 Card
home country: Denmark • living/working in Copenhagen, Denmark
fax: +45 3295 2321 • email: 2gd@2gd.dk • url: http://www.2gd.dk
date of birth / date of foundation: Jan Nielsen 21/09/68 / Ole Lund 14/03/66 / 2GD 01/06/96
CV / short company history/ studies/ education: Graphic designers Jan Nielsen and Ole Lund, both graduates from The Danish School of Contemporary Design, established the 2GD-studio in 1996. Before setting up their own studio, they made contact with strong and influential design studios inside Denmark as well as abroad. Jan Nielsen has prior to graduation in 1995 studied at the Gerrit Rietveld Academy in Amsterdam and School of Visual Arts in New York. Ole Lund has prior to his graduation undertaken studies at the Art Center College of Design, Vevey and The Royal College of Art in London, also having received training from Pentagram Design Inc. in New York. Both have contributed as designers at Eleven Danes Design, Kontrapunkt, and Christian Bjørn Design in Copenhagen. The 2GD portfolio includes among other works, designs for The PTT Museum, EMI, the Foss Corporation, Sony Nordic, BOBLBEE, Carlsberg Breweries, Danish National Radio, Bruuns Bazaar, The Danish National Railway Agency, Blizzard, Kirk and Tag Heuer. The 2GD-works has been acknowledged among others by The Danish Design Center, which threefold has awarded 2GD the IG-prize. Twice 2GD have received the Guldkorn Award for their contribution to the field of Advertising and Design, and one Good Design Award from The Chicago Athenaeum.
Do the landscapes/dark winters/midsummer nights have an effect on your soul and design? Maybe indirectly. What influence have traditional folkloristic art and pop art on your work? Design may not be art. But if designers do not approach it with the passion of an artist, stretch towards the light and fumble after what lies hidden on the top shelf, who in the process will? What would you do if you were not a designer? It is a very abstract question because we love our profession, but I think it would be something about creating e.g. Gardner or another profession where every detail matters. Do you feel, there is a Scandinavian (design) identity or special approach? Yes - we live in a very peaceful part of the world - Scandinavian design is very peaceful. What are your inspirations, aims, dreams and what's your philosophy? We base our work on an ideology that views style as the surface of meaning, and meaning as the essence of style. This two-sided strategy directs itself toward the visual esthetic of the surface, its signals and expressions. As well as the involvement and awareness of the client in the definition of the substance of the identity we jointly create.

A2-GRAPHIC

Scott Williams / Henrik Kubel
artworks on page: 050/051 Logo, 141 Typefaces, 149 Experimental typefaces
home Country: England / Denmark • living/working in London, England
fax: +44 207 739 4541 • email: info@a2-graphics.co.uk • url: www.a2-graphics.co.uk
date of birth / date of foundation: A2-GRAPHICS/SW/HK, London founded in 1999
principal partners: Scott Williams 1976, Henrik Kubel 1972
CV / short company history/ studies/ education: A2-GRAPHICS/SW/HK was formed in 1999 by partners, Scott Williams and Henrik Kubel, whilst studying at the Royal College of Art, London. As a design collaborative we have been working professionally in London for the past three years, and are working for a number of arts/cultural organisations including The British Council, the V&A Museum, Cubitt Gallery, 1508.dk and Aveny-T Theatre, to name a few. As a graphic design consultancy A2-GRAPHICS/SW/HK encompasses corporate identity, publication design, typography, exhibition signage, poster design and new media. An integral part of our practice is typography - both its design and eventual treatment.
latest personal / commercial projects: A series of posters for the Theatre Aveny-T, a catalogue for the British Council Touring exhibition 'Multiplication', a corporate identity and typeface design for the Danish Government Modernising Programme,a letterpress poster for Buckinghamshire Chiltern University College, a series of e-mail invitations for Cubitt Gallery.
Do the landscapes/dark winters/midsummer nights have an effect on your soul and design? Kubel: I work more and longer hours during the winter, soul wise I prefer the summer... What influence have traditional folkloristic art and pop art on your work? Kubel: I guess that pop art made some impact on me as I was growing up (and when I designed the logo for www.fontyoufonts.com). Today, most things can inspire me, that be the people on the street, the woodletters in our studio, the smell of paint at the silkscreen workshop as well as a tray of Baskerville...what surrounds me really...the sound of silence... What would you do if you were not a designer? Williams: No idea. Kubel: I guess that I would be an artist. Do you feel, there is a Scandinavian (design) identity or special approach? Kubel: Not really, the world is getting smaller. The magazine Wallpaper is trying to showcase 'the scandinavian way of seeing, living and designing!', probably as close as you will get to the question... What are your inspirations, aims, dreams and what's your philosophy? Inspirations: Not quantifiable. Aim: To be recognised for our work. Philosophy: To make typeface design an integrated part of every design solution. Dream: Kubel: To produce more posters in letterpress, ...and some day to get paid properly for all the hard work and many hours we spend on producing work for clients with too small budgets... And to set up a design studio in New York.

ÅBÄKE

artworks on page: 188/189 Sketch book - images
home country: Sweden, France, Wales • living/working in London, England
fax : +44 207 249 23 80 • email: a.b.a.k.e@free.fr
date of foundation: Summer 2000
CV / short company history/ studies/ education & latest personal / commercial projects: Åbäke studied graphic design and illustration BA and MA in Brighton University, École Nationale supérieure des Arts décoratifs (Paris, France), Högskolan för Design och Konsthantverk (Gothenburg, Sweden), SVA (New York, USA), Taike - University of Art & Design (Helsinki, Finland), Central St Martins (London), Royal College of Art (London). Åbäke works with and for: Singers, Bands, Artists, Universities, Architects, Streetwear companies, Furniture designers, Fashion designers, Curators, Clubs, Record labels, design publications, Magazines, Councils, Dance teachers, Video commisioners. They are called: A Camp, Air, Daftpunk, Righteousboy, Cilla Blomqvist, Kenji Yanobe, Creativebase, ENSAD, Camberwell, Generic costume, Kitsune, Clive Sall, Martino Gamper, Rainer Spehl, Peter Jensen, Gaspard Yurkievich, Scarlet, Sexymachinery, Source UK, Etienne Daho, Virgin France, Dazed & Confused, Bettina komenda, Nigel Coates, Maison Martin Margiela, The British Council.

Do the landscapes/dark winters/midsummer nights have an effect on your soul and design? Last summer we had tomato plants in our studio, we grew them from the seeds, they became 2 metres high and produced beautiful tomatoes for us to have for lunch. This seasons tomatoes are currently 8 centimeteres high, and growing. What influence have traditional folkloristic art and pop art on your work? We are currently designing the printed material for the european latin american dance championship. What would you do if you were not a designer? A friend of ours needed a bed. Its construction was "dramatised" and filmed for a pop promo we directed. Do you feel, there is a Scandinavian (design) identity or special approach? We sent a project about pre-conceived ideas of finnish people to finnish guys we met in switzerland. 2 months later, they e-mailed they learnt a lot about themselves. What are your inspirations, aims, dreams and what's your philosophy? All of the above.

ACNE

artworks on page: 104/105 Selfpromotion »Family«, 106/107 Acne-Jeans I Netbaby - images
home country: Sweden • living/working in Stockholm, Sweden
fax: +46 8 55579999 • email: contact@acne.se • url: www.acne.se
date of foundation: 1996
CV / short company history/ studies/ education: ACNE was founded in 1996 as a design agency with the ambition of developing own brands and products as well as helping to build other people's brands. ACNE works within the fields of fashion, entertainment and technology.
latest personal / commercial projects: X
Do the landscapes/dark winters/midsummer nights have an effect on your soul and design? Yes and No. What influence have traditional folkloristic art and pop art on your work? You tell us. (...forget it! dgv.) What would you do if you were not a designer? Don't know. Do you feel, there is a Scandinavian (design) identity or special approach? No. What are your inspirations, aims, dreams and what's your philosophy? Lust, knowledge, anarchy.

AGUST AEVAR GUNNARSSON

artworks on page: 119 CD cover »Sigur Ros« - images 120 CD Cover »Barry Adamson + Pan Sonic«
home country: Iceland • living/working in Reykjavik, Iceland
email: gusturinn@isholf.is
date of birth: 22./09/1976
CV / short company history/ studies/ education: Iethnskólinn í Reykjavík (1997), Listaháskólinn Íslands (2002). Music: Von (1997), Von-brigiethi/Recycle bin (1998), Ágætis byrjun (1999).
latest personal / commercial projects:: my latest work is my graduate-prodject and is made for TV. It is a kind of music-video.
Do the landscapes/dark winters/midsummer nights have an effect on your soul and design? With out doubt it has major effect on my soul. If this effect reflects in my work is hard to say. What influence have traditional folkloristic art and pop art on your work? Pop is my fountain. What would you do if you were not a designer? I would be a fulltime musician. Do you feel, there is a Scandinavian (design) identity or special approach? I don't consider myself as a scandinavian in any way but I am sure that the surrounding has an effect on your work. So those who life in the Scandianavian area must have some specialty in there identity or approach. What are your inspirations, aims, dreams and what's your philosophy? My inspirations comes from every direction and sometimes it is harder to block them out then to accept them and I can imagien how hard it must be in a faster community. My aim is to make this community a better place before I leave, this I try to do in my every act. When I say better I mean more open minded ...

ALPHABETICAL ORDER

artworks on page: 050/051 Illustrations I Logos, 070/071 Press image »This is Alphabetical Order«, 072/073 Press image, 112 Catalogue - image, 134 Illustration, 144 Image »Arrows«
home country: Sweden • living/working in Stockholm, Sweden
fax: +46 8 55 60 78 78
email: everyone@alphabeticalorder.com • url: www.alphabeticalorder.com
date of foundation: 01/06/01
latest personal / commercial projects: Furnishing our studio (which has showed to be a real sisyphos task). / Pressmaterial for an exhibition called "Sweden Scores" in Los Angeles, U.S.A. Commissioned by the Consulate of Sweden.
Do the landscapes/dark winters/midsummer nights have an effect on your soul and design? Yes, it's easier to be productive during spring/summertime. What influence have traditional folkloristic art and pop art on your work? It makes us dizzy. What would you do if you were not a designer? Marcus: I would be a teacher! Johan: I would be a retired professional skateboarder! Daniel: I keep telling you people, I AM NOT A DESIGNER! Do you feel, there is a Scandinavian (design) identity or special approach? No, this 20–30 male design looks pretty much the same all over the world. Age and gender have a much greater influence on the output of your work than geography. What are your inspirations, aims, dreams and what's your philosophy? Combining post–consumerism advertising and aesthethics. Alphabetical Order, building a better tomorrow!

AKAY

artworks on page: 142/143 »Akayism« photos + images
home country: Sweden • living/working not only in Stockholm, Sweden
email: info@akayism.org • url: www.akayism.org
date of birth: between 1965 and 1975
latest personal / commercial projects: citysleepers in tokyo
Do the landscapes/dark winters/midsummer nights have an effect on your soul and design? No, just on my ability to work outside. What influence have traditional folkloristic art and pop art on your work? I'm not interested in pop art, but folkart is always interesting, even more if its stuff that has been produced without the idea of being art. What would you do if you were not a designer? I'm not a designer. Do you feel, there is a Scandinavian (design) identity or special approach? I'm not into this design thing at all, I have no clue what other people are doing or what makes them look alike, probably cos somebody developed something or have a very specific style and everybody else biting his or her style. Hahaha! What are your inspirations, aims, dreams and what's your philosophy? Inspiration: photos, tags, zevs, clean walls, barbara kruger, jenny holzer, allen wexler, adams, fluxus, evation (book), kp, unik. aims and dreams: do more... and better. philosophy: time to redefine crime.

ANNE-LI KARLSSON

artworks on page: 134 Illustrations, 167 Illustration »Köttresan«, 176 Illustrations
home country: Sweden • living/working in Stockholm, Sweden
email: anne_li@bboy.com
date of birth / date of foundation: born 1970, established since 1998
CV / short company history/ studies/ education: I made my first illustration for Darling - 98. The theme was porn and together with violance it turned out to be my niche as an illustrator. Also useful for sexual instruction and I´ve been involved in two book projects on that issue; "Woman health" and "What a young man should know". Did a series of illustrations for Dagens Nyheter and was rewarded with a silver medal in the Society of News Design´s annual competition 2001. Parallel with work I´ve been educating myself at Konstfack. I´ve been spending time in Tokyo and San Francisco and plan to spend the next two years in San Francisco.
latest personal / commercial projects: A book project; Woman health for Bonnier förlag
Do the landscapes/dark winters/midsummer nights have an effect on your soul and design? It gives me a nice touch of manic-depression. What influence have traditional folkloristic art and pop art on your work? Not much, I´m more influenced by my moms lack of taste. What would you do if you were not a designer? Push Snickers in a kiosk at the central station. Do you feel, there is a Scandinavian (design) identity or special approach? Isn´t it Swiss? What are your inspirations, aims, dreams and what's your philosophy? Worlddomiantion!

ANNI VESTERGAARD / KARIN VON SCHANTZ

artworks on page: 190 Web site »POL-365« - screens
home country: Denmark / Denmark-Finland • living/working in Copenhagen, Denmark
email: anni_vestergaard@hotmail.com / von-schantz@wanadoo.dk
date of birth: 23/01/72 / 26/08/69
CV / short company history/ studies/ education: Anni > Graphic designer from The Danish School of Design, Institute of Visual Communication; Karin > BA dramaturgy/ classical studies University of Copenhagen, Graphic designer from The Danish School of Design, Institute of Visual Communication, guest-year at Institute og Textile and product
latest personal / commercial projects: Anni > magazine layout > rart (co-orporation with sidsel stubbe). identity for fashionlabel > eksempel (co-orporation with pulsk ravn), identity for arcitect + graphic company > jyllnor & rohweder; Karin > identity for bellydancer-duo, identity for Nagoya University of Art and science for Kontrapunkt A/S, identity and homepage for a new publishers network association, patterns for textile industry, 10 paperbacks, campaign for better work-environment in supermarkets.
Do the landscapes/dark winters/midsummer nights have an effect on your soul and design? Anni: Since the weather has a big influence on your mood and the mood you are in affects your design, I suppose yes, in a way... Karin: YES! Epecially on my productivity! What influence have traditional folkloristic art and pop art on your work? Both: Daily life more than art is really what influenced "POL-365". When working with "POL-365" Danish rituals, habits, ways of communicating and typical daily objects were our major influences. They all partake in creating intertextuality between everyday-life and "POL-365". Rather than folkloristic art and pop art our project is inspired by the Danish tradition for a humanistic anddemocratic approach to life." What would you do if you were not a designer? Anni: Cook. Karin: I have volunteered in summercamps for Russian orphans, and that is what I would do all year if I wasn´t a designer. Do you feel, there is a Scandinavian (design) identity or special approach? Anni: Yes. Karin: I guess Scandinavian design is about simplicity, reflection, a democratic approach, functionalism and respect for materials. Some of these principles could need a make-over, some of them better never go away! What are your inspirations, aims, dreams and what's your philosophy? Anni: Everyday life. Karin: OOh - I get too inspired by everything...The eternal conflict between being open and getting lots of ideas and actually carry them out! My "philosophy" and aim: Keeping an open mind, improve yourself and the way you act in this world, respect other people. (My secret dream: Being un-materialistic, which is hard when you´re a designer!!)

ANNLAUG AUESTAD / STAVANGERILLUSTRATØRENE

artworks on page: 185 Book illustrations
home country: Norway • living/working in Stavanger, Norway
fax: +47 51 91 68 06
email: annlaug@stavanger-illustratorene.no • url: www.stavanger-illustratorene.no
date of birth: 06/10/65
CV / short company history/ studies/ education: We are a graphic design studio specialising in illustration. We receive commissions from both arts and business sectors and have carried out work for design companies, advertising agencies, book and magazine publishers, theatre companies, educational institutions, charitable organisations and private companies. Books, magazines, catalogues, brochures, folders, corporate identities, web sites and signage programmes are just some of the things that we have been asked to work on. studies/ education: National college of art and design in Bergen, Norway
latest personal / commercial projects: Children book: "Hugo and the lawn mover"
Do the landscapes/dark winters/midsummer nights have an effect on your soul and design? Let me put it this way: The culture, my childhood and the early interest for drawing and painting is important for my art work today. The landscape, the nature and the Nordic light have also effected my soul, and the person I am to day - and my visual art work. What influence have traditional folkloristic art and pop art on your work? I think the traditional folkloristic art and also pop art is both inspiration for my work and the visual expression. What would you do if you were not a designer? Maybe a baker, or maybe something with horses.

ÁRMANN AGNARSSON

artworks on page: 136 Poster, 186 Poster, 187 Illustrations
home country: Iceland • living/working in Reykjavik, Iceland
email: ami@lhi.is / armanna@hotmail.com
date of birth: 26/04/1974
CV / Short history / studies / education: Reykjavik Technical School – Prepress, Iceland Academy of Arts – LHI, Grapfic design – LHI, 1997–1999: Morgunbladid – Newspaper, 1999-2001: Xyzeta Adagency, 2001: Deluxe Adagency
Latest personal/commercial projects: Exhibitions: SIE Project, Laugavegur / The Strokes concert Iceland.
Do the landscapes/dark winters/midsummer nights have an effect on your soul and design? Definitely – depression vs happiness – short vs long. What influences have traditional folkloristic art and pop art on your work? Hhumm – can't really say. What would you do if you were not a designer? Assistant designer with attitude problems. Do you feel there is a scandinavian (design) identity or special approach? Not really. What are your inspirations, aims, dreams and what's your philosphy? Always: School, LHI, hin Fjögur Fræknu, music, people, art, films, competition, Dieter, my 3's and numer one. At the moment: Dieter Roth, futura 2000, Richard Hamilton, Hjalti&Sagmeister, Herbert, Morr, Yo La Tengo, Múm. Aims, dreams and philosophy: learn, progress, dream.

BENNY BOX DESIGN

artworks on page: 050/051 Logo, 082/083 Graphic experiments, 084 Magazine cover, 085 + 086/087 Graphic experiments, 168 Illustration, 185 Flash game setting
home country: Denmark • living/working in Copenhagen, Denmark
email: bennybox@bennybox.dk • url: www.bennybox.dk
date of birth / date of foundation: Rune Fisker: 1974 / Esben Fisker: 1976 / Benny Box: 2000
CV / short company history/ studies/ education: Benny Box design was started in 2000. In the beginning we did mostly Illustrations for magazines and other types of illustration related work, but we have gradually broadened our workarea, to include other types of assignments, such as: production design, flash presentations, animation design and web design. We are trying to use our unique style in all our work, and not be a "we can do anything, and adapt to any style" kind of company.
latest personal / commercial projects:We are starting work on a pilot episode for an animated tv-serie for children. It is a cell-shaded 3D animated serie, and we are both really excited about it! We have, for some time now, been working on a publication/combilation of graphic novels called "Puhakirja". Our aim is to publish a new issue every 3-4 months.
Do the landscapes/dark winters/midsummer nights have an effect on your soul and design? Most of the time the Danish weather is fantasticly depressing, cloudy, rainy, windy. The kind of weather that makes you reach deep into the dark pits of your soul and make really trashy design, and when summer comes you get really happy and want to use lots of bright colours. The colors of Denmark, and also the rest of scandinavia has a certain mood to it, that is really inspiring. But sometimes you have to seek the opposite of your surroundings, and the opposite of what you are used to doing; so we try to be inspired by other countries and cultures too. What influence have traditional folkloristic art and pop art on your work? I wouldn't say that traditional folkloristic danish art have influenced our approch to design and illustration. These days, the modern art scene in Copenhagen and other Scandinavian cities are a great source for inspiration. The great thing about looking at art, is the freedom you can sense in the works. Graphic design is more restricted because of its comercial nature. What would you do if you were not a designer? Rune:

I have always wanted to be a designer/illustrator so I have never really considerd another career. but from the top of my head I would say astronaut, or maybe professional surfer. Esben: Probably out of work. I spent so much time drawing as a kid, that I don't have any other interests or talents. Do you feel, there is a Scandinavian (design) identity or special approach? There is a very strong Scandinavian design identity, and especially Denmark is well known for its simple and minimalistic design. I believe that many scandinavian designers has a lot of personality in their design too. But in the area of illustration, I think the other scandinavian countries has a lot of great artists, and Denmark is kind of lacking behind. The rainnesance of illustration, that we have seen in the rest of the world, hasn't really happened in Denmark yet. What are your inspirations, aims, dreams and what's your philosophy? Rune: I'm inspired by a lot of different visual fields, from comics to graphic design, and illustration. And of course music, probably my greatest source of inspiration. Esben: My inspirations change all the time, but I respect the works of people that has personality in what they do. I try to get inspired by lots of different genres, not just graphic design and illustration.

We believe that we have something unique to offer, and that it is very importaint to hold on to this uniqueness. The trends of the graphic design world changes so fast these days, and too many designers forget themself trying to adapt to the next hip thing. How are you going to convince clients that they should use you, if you are just doing the same as everybody else? Off course designers must move on all the time, but not at the expense of their personal style. Our aim is to always experiment with new ways of expressing ourselves visually, and never be content with the way our works looks. Our dream is to keep doing this until we are dead (and maybe beyond).

BLEED DESIGNSTUDIO

artworks on page: 068 Image »Reject«, 069 Image, 110 Selfpromotion - posters
home country: Norway • living/working in Oslo, Norway
fax: +47 22809971 • email: bleed@bleed.no • url: www.bleed.no
date of foundation: June 2000
CV / short company history/ studies/ education: Bleeds main focus is graphic design as a communication tool. Bleed develops innovative design solutions for all medias/channels and has won prices for projects in both traditional and new medias. Bleed offers design services in interactive design, graphic design, animations, consept thinking, strategy, project management and programming.
latest personal / commercial projects: www.smirnoff-ice.net, www.zaplife.com, FJORDS magazine, www.fjordsmagazine.com, www.bleed.no/hunting, Øyafestivalen (Øya Music festival), Platekompaniet (print, web, tv animations)
Do the landscapes/dark winters/midsummer nights have an effect on your soul and design? The main advantage of winter is that you get more work done... The dark and cold days and nights makes indoor life more inviting. Scandinavian design often are clean and at the same time warm... this could off course have something to do with winter, indoor life, wall to wall carpeting and a fireplace, but I wont speculate.... What influence have traditional folkloristic art and pop art on your work? I don´t believe in folklore, but pop art have always influenced design and I think the other way around... art is weak... no challenge there... What would you do if you were not a designer? artist... or walking the streets aimlessly... Do you feel, there is a Scandinavian (design) identity or special approach? Scandinavian design definitely have its own expression. I don´t think it have anything to do with the work approach, but more culture and history. What are your inspirations, aims, dreams and what's your philosophy? Inspiration: Life. Aim: Be happy. Dream: Be even more happy. Philosophy: define, develop, delight and decay.

BURNFIELD

artworks on page: 046 Web site I Illustrations
home country: Sweden • living/working in Stockholm, Sweden
email: do@burnfield.com • url: www.burnfield.com
date of foundation: y2k
CV / short company history/ studies/ education: burnfield are the brothers peter & martin ström, who mostley create cute animals and other stuff of educational value. ps. we don't smoke.
Do the landscapes/dark winters/midsummer nights have an effect on your soul and design? Yes, especially the traditionally rostraces at midnight during summertime. What influence have traditional folkloristic art and pop art on your work? We love the Muppets. What would you do if you were not a designer? Live with mum. Do you feel, there is a Scandinavian (design) identity or special approach? Yes, and it must have to do with all that drinking and depression. from all that darkness outside all the time comes depression, and depression is good for creativity. But be careful - it might kill you. What are your inspirations, aims, dreams and what's your philosophy? To make the world a better place, and as long as there are people like bush and sharon we have a long journey ahead. and we love the Muppets.

CAMILLA IRMELIN MYKLEBUST / STAVANGERILLUSTRATØRENE

artworks on page: 080/081 Illustration »Oil industry«, 168 Illustration »Drinking«, 169 Illustration »Summer Holiday«
home country: Norway • living/working in Stavanger, Norway
fax: +47 51 91 68 06
email: camilla@stavanger-illustratorene.no • url: www.stavanger-illustratorene.no
date of birth: 27/07/1974
CV / short company history/ studies/ education: I´ve got two different establish grants, to set up in business. One stately and one from an organization in Norway, Grafill, which is for Graphic Designers and Illustrators. My company is now about 2-3 years old since I´ve started it, at first I sat at home, and then we got together as "Stavangerillustratørene", were there are 4 of us, everyone working freelance. Of studies/education I have 2 years of Visual Communication Design in Norway (Forus Videregående skole), 3 years of Visual Communication Design, specialicing in General Illustration in England, BA Hons(Middlesex University). I´ve also participated in an exhibition with a big oilpastel- drawing in London at The Mall Galleries when I was a student there.
latest personal / commercial projects: I´m participating in a common exhibition in a Gallery called Neo in Stavanger.
Do the landscapes/dark winters/midsummer nights have an effect on your soul and design? I don´t really get that effected by it, because when I´m working, it all depends on what the projects are..But I think the way I work, my influences are a mixture of different things, as growing up, heritage- interests, everything that´s around me on a daily basis, humdrum stuff, sometimes boring things, sometimes happy things... What would you do if you were not a designer? If I were not an Illustrator, I would like to be a singer or a dancer, or maybe travelling around doing stand-up comedy..

CAOZ

artworks on page: 050/051 Logo, Web site »Caoz«,
home country: Iceland • living/working in Reykjavik, Iceland
fax: +354 511 3551 • email: info@caoz.is • url: www.caoz.com
date of foundation: 01/02/2001
CV / short company history/ studies/ education: The Graphic Department at OZ was turned to a spin-out company to be able to carry out assignments from outside of OZ. We also gathered more excellent designers and animators right from the beginning to form CAOZ.
latest personal / commercial projects: We are now working on an animated film for children (cartoon), The lost little Caterpillar (www.thecaterpillar.com), heavy process and very promishing. Also we are designing graphics for local television station. Also we have been working on a website for a great designer (www.michael-young.com). We are working on a re-design of a local brand of soft drinks. The focus is on children and we have made new packeting and three animated tv ads. ... and more

Do the landscapes/dark winters/midsummer nights have an effect on your soul and design? Yes, it must be, but in what way I don't know. The contrast in light between winter and summer is enourmus and it must show in our work. What influence have traditional folkloristic art and pop art on your work? Well, we don't have much heritage regarding visual art here in Iceland. I guess for most of us in Iceland, we look very much to other countries. We are done with Brody and Carson. Many designers here are influenced with what is going on rihgt now in Europe. But to me it's imitation. For myself I just want to set my own rules and carry them out. If an element in my design does not make it better, then it has not earned it's existance, out with it. So cutting away everything unnecessary is my rule. May sound cold and engineered, and it also may be the first sign of a die-ing designer... who knows. What would you do if you were not a designer? Sail the big round on a sailboat. Do you feel, there is a Scandinavian (design) identity or special approach? Yes, deffenately. I'm not sure how to describe it. Once I spoke to a very good Deutch designer. He did not see their style from another... to me the difference is obvious. I guess that Scandinavian style is still living in the sixties. It's light, clean, constructive and minimal. Perhaps this is just my whish. What are your inspirations, aims, dreams and what's your philosophy? Life is my inspiration (cliché?) but I get ideas everywhere, in my dreams, Tom & Jerry, landscape, architecture... My aim... I want to move more into motion graphics, on web, on TV... but I am constantly struggeling with the question "why?"... why this, why that, why am I doing this, why am I a graphic designer... why is this working? Less is more... Why? Why me?

CLEA SIMONSEN

artworks on page: 141 »Domino«, 210 Illustration
home country: Denmark • living/working in Chicago, USA/Berlin, Germany
email: clea@cleas.dk • url: www.cleas.dk
date of birth: 30/06/73, date of foundation: January 2000 (start freelancing)
CV / short company history/ studies/ education: Work experience > Jan 2002 – present: freelance employed graphic designer by Heute Morgen Grafik, Berlin, Jan. 2000 – present: self-employed graphic designer and illustrator in Copenhagen and Berlin. Education: 1994 – 1999: Danmarks Designskole, Copenhagen; Degree project: Einstein's Dreams – the use of time in visual communication, based on my theoretical studies at the Glasgow School of Art. 1998 – 1999: studies at the Glasgow School of Art, Scotland; The Master's Degree of Design Programme dissertation: Time in Visual Communication – a comparison between the film, the book and the poster. 1993 – 1994: studies at The Heatherley School of Fine Art, London.
Latest personal / commercial projects: Flur-online – website for Flur (gallery), Berlin; Das Orchester, Jean Anouilh – flyer/programme for Theater am Ufer, Berlin; Diktierstube – sprechen Sie jetzt (theatre), flyer/poster for Kunsthaus Tacheles, Berlin
Do the landscapes/dark winters/midsummer nights have an effect on your soul and design? Winter depressions are hard to avoid but forgotten in the summer nights. I cannot say that this has a specific effect on my work. I haven't analysed it. What influence have traditional folkloristic art and pop art on your work? No great influence – at least none that I am aware of. I am inspired by anti-design/non-design and ugliness, but that's different. (There is too much design in this world. It makes me feel tired and overwhelmed.) What would you do if you were not a designer? This is indeed a strange job, and a job without much meaning (adding to the winter depression). I would open a cat pension or fight for animal rights. This sounds pretentious but it is the first thing that comes to my mind. I am very happy as a graphic designer. When I work I forget to eat and to go out. Do you feel, there is a Scandinavian (design) identity or special approach? I think there is a Scandinavian design identity and Living abroad makes it clearer to me. Many good things can be said and many of the clichés can be repeated; we are thorough intellectual and honest, we are aesthetes and humanists. But we suffer from an extraordinary mixture of megalomania and low self-esteem. Convinced of our own superiority we risk becoming arrogant, negative and too serious. At the same time we are unnaturally impressed by foreign design schools and particularly by foreign recognition of Danish design. This cannot be healthy. It is very provincial. What are your inspirations, aims, dreams and what's your philosophy? I am interested in the field between graphic design and fine art and I am interested in the idea of anti-design and understatement. I am interested in art presented and disguised as graphic design and in design presented as art. As a graphic designer I ask myself what part I should be playing and how visible I should be. Am I a mere servant (communicating for someone else) or could I be more? Is it interesting for me to be more? Am I allowed to be more without going all the way and become an artist? Hopefully I will always be able to work on good projects with good people who understand and share my ideas. This is all a graphic designer can hope for?

DAGNY REYKJALIN

artworks on page: 118 Poster
home country: Iceland • living/working in Reykjavik, Iceland
email: dagny@reykjalin.com • url: http://www.reykjalin.com
date of birth: 29/04/1978
CV / short company history/ studies/ education: Currently a student of graphic design at Iceland Academy of the Arts. Working as a freelance designer.
latest personal / commercial projects: Designing and building a website for the department of design and architecture at Iceland Academy of the Arts. I'm also part of INT, the Icelandic National Team. We are setting up a portal for art and design in iceland and around the world.
Do the landscapes/dark winters/midsummer nights have an effect on our soul and design? Yes, most definitely. They have deep effect on my personality and I want to think that my personality is reflected in my work. The best parties are also in the sunshine at midnight! What influence have traditional folkloristic art and pop art on your work? I believe they have more influence than I think. Being local is considered tacky and everybody want to be global, but when everybody become so alike, the best source for something new is in your local environment and history. Like for example Sigur Rós, the Icelandic band. What would you do if you were not a designer? This is a tough one, I think i'd be in visual arts; painting or graphic arts, or atleast I think I'd end up there. Do you feel, there is a Scandinavian (design) identity or special approach? I think graphic design is alot reflected by other classical interior design from Scandinavia as being friendly and reflecting prosperity of the society. But with the whole globalisation the line is really blurry. What are your inspirations, aims, dreams and what's your philosophy? My aim is to be true to myself in my works, ofcourse i dream of being successful in whatever I will embark but also and not the least to be proud of what I do.

DAGUR HILMARSSON

Gott folk McCann–Erickson and Fiskar
artworks on page: 128/129 Images
home country: Iceland • living/working in Reykjavik, Iceland
fax: +354 5 700 270 • email: dagur@gottfolk.is • url: www.fiskar.is and www.gottfolk.is
date of birth: 11/07/1966
CV / short company history/ studies/ education: 1990-1994 worked as an assistant designer at Argus Advertising Agency. 1991-1995 studied art at The Icelandic School of Arts and Crafts and graduated as a Graphic Designer in 1995. 1995 founded a design-house, Myndasmidja Austurbaejar (East End Image Factory) with collegue and friend, Borkur Arnarson. 1996 December 1st, MA (EEIF) joined Gott folk (later Gott folk McCann-Erickson). 1996-2000 worked as a senior designer and later art director at Gott folk Advertising Agency. 2000-2001 started a multimedia divison inside Gott folk; Fiskar www.fiskar.is - and worked there as an art director. Since August 2001 I have worked as a Design Director for Gott folk McCann-Erickson and Fiskar.
latest personal / commercial projects: I am working a lot for Coca-Cola these days, preparing for their Summer campaign. A long with that I'm designing a corporate identity for a low-priced drug store chain, amongst various other things.
Do the landscapes/dark winters/midsummer nights have an effect on your soul and design? To be honest, having this spectacular landscape just outside my door, I think I sometimes take it for granted. Maybe the landscape has more impact on my work than I realize? But yes, it definately softens my soul and mind to be out there in nature. A lot of people here in Iceland find the long dark winter days to be depressing but I have always liked it. It is good to concentrate on your work when the days are darker. In the summertime I love to recharge my batteries by spending more time with my kids. What influence have traditional folkloristic art and pop art on your work? Not more than any other factor in my life. What would you do if you were not a designer? I would probably be a writer or somewhere in the field of helping people in need, disabled people or alcoholics for example. Do you feel, there is a Scandinavian (design) identity or special approach? Yes, I think Scandinavian graphic design is often light and safe compared to other nations. Maybe it has something to do with the way we look - in general? What are your inspirations, aims, dreams and what's your philosophy? I guess I could say that little incidents are my biggest inspirations. It might be some things my kids say or do or some line in a song. A part of a poem I read or just seeing the sun go down. Even a stranger on the street with his behaviour can inspire me in my works. My aims: To become a better person (in all it's sense) today then I was yesterday. Dreams: That I'll live to see my kids grow old and happy. Philosophy: Make peace with your self and the world will follow.

EGILL HARDAR

artworks on page: 116/117 Images
home country: Iceland • living/working in Reykjavik, Iceland
email: egillhar@simnet.is • url: www.egillhardar.com
date of foundation: 1998
CV / short company history/ studies/ education: B.A. in fine arts from the Icelandic Academy of the arts. Worked for Gagarin Ltd., Fiskar and teaching multimedia. latest personal / commercial projects: www.egillhardar.com
Do the landscapes/dark winters/midsummer nights have an effect on your soul and design? Yes. Mostly on my soul though. What influence have traditional folkloristic art and pop art on your work? None. My influenes come mostly from the web and books and stuff. What would you do if you were not a designer? Artist of any kind. Do you feel, there is a Scandinavian (design) identity or special approach? Not really. Though scandinavians have a more "laid back" approach to things. What are your inspirations, aims, dreams and what's your philosophy? I want to be famous for something but not rich. My philosophy is to be kind to everyone and basicly have a good time living life.

EKHORNFORSS / NON-FORMAT

artworks on page: 012 poster CD cover I Entry call for CD compilation, 023 Fashion images I CD cover, 064 CD cover, 083 Illustration, 126/127 CD booklet - image
home country: Norway / UK • living/working in London, England
email: info@ekhornforss.com • url: www. non-format.com
date of foundation: 2000
CV / short company history/ studies/ education: Both EkhornForss and Non-Format were formed in London by Kjell Ekhorn and Jon Forss in 2000 to colaborate on print design projects for the publishing and music industries. In 2001 EkhornForss Limited was established and in the same year they were nominated for best design team in Music Week's Creative and design Awards.
latest personal / commercial projects: EkhornForss: 1. continue art directing the London based music magazine The Wire; 2. has just completed the design of a coffee table book celebrating the 500 greatest singles / Non-Format: 1. designs for various music packaging projects; 2. currently working on product design for a Canadian feature film.
Do the landscapes/dark winters/midsummer nights have an effect on your soul and design? It has made us embrace everything urban and concrete but we always look forward to putting the clocks back one hour. What influence have traditional folkloristic art and pop art on your work? Pop art is the main reason why we got into graphics, traditional folklore art is a good reason to stay there.. What would you do if you were not a designer? Sell our Letraset collection. Do you feel, there is a Scandinavian (design) identity or special approach? Hope not. What are your inspirations, aims, dreams and what's your philosophy? Inspirations: fashion/fiction/music/film/photography and fresh snow on concrete structure. Aims: we aim to surprise. Dreams: big in Japan/penthouse in Sapporo. Philosophy: good design > mass market > cliché > embarrassment > "it's over" > fetish > revival > interesting > style > good design > mass market > cliché > embarrassment > "it's over" > fetish > revival > interesting > style > good design > mass market > cliché > embarrassment > "it's over" > fetish > revival > interesting > style > good design > mass market > cliché > embarrassment > "it's over" > fetish > revival > interesting > style > good design > mass market > cliché > embarrassment > "it's over" > fetish > revival > interesting > style > good design...

ELIN KJØSNES / STAVANGERILLUSTRATØRENE

artworks on page: 168 Illustrations »Summer« I »Rabitt and Cowboy«
home country: Norway • living/working in Stavanger, Norway
fax: +47 51 91 68 06
email: elin@stavanger-illustratorene.no • url: www.stavanger-illustratorene.no
date of birth: 19/05/1974
CV / short company history/ studies/ education: 1995 - 1998: BA Visual Communication, Illustration, Kent Institute of Art and Design, England. 1993 - 1995: Visual Communication and drawing, Forus vgs., Norway. In august 1998 I startet to work as an freelance illustrator. In December 2000 I came in contact with the other illustrators that now is Stavanger-illustratørene, and I became a part of them in May 2001.
latest personal / commercial projects: Magazine-illustration for Reklameetasjen (Stavanger), Layout, English grammy, Det Norske Samlaget, Illustrations to a oil-company BP, about safety on the platform, Blå (Stavanger)
Do the landscapes/dark winters/midsummer nights have an effect on your soul and design? I like the contrast from winter to summer, the change of color give inspiration. What would you do if you were not a designer? I think I would like to be a farmer. What are your inspirations, aims, dreams and what's your philosophy? I get my inspirations from everyday elements and happenings around me.

E-TYPES

artworks on page: 008 poster, 025 Logo in Café, 050/051 Logo, 056/057 Catalogue covers, 101 Film magazine cover
home country: Denmark • living/working in Copenhagen, Denmark
fax: +45 332 545 00 • email: info@e-types.com • url: www.e-types.com
Date of foundation: 1997

FELLOW DESIGNERS

artworks on page: 036 poster, 099 Exhibition poster, 100 Poster »Adidas«, 103 Movie poster
Home country:Sweden • living/working in Stockholm, Sweden
fax: +46 8 31 24 10 • email: paul@fellowdesigners.com • url: www.fellowdesigners.com
date of foundation: 01/09/1997
CV / short company history/ studies/ education: Fellow designers is Eva Liljefors and Paul Kühlhorn. We graduated 1997, Paul from Konstfack University of Arts, Crafts and Design and Eva from Beckmans school of design (both located in Stockholm). We started our business during our last year in school. We work with corporate identities, logotypes, posters for exhibitions, movies and theatres, illustrations etc. We always work as a team.
latest personal / commercial projects: Poster and titles for Memfis film, "Lilja 4-ever" movie by Lukas Moodysson.
Do the landscapes/dark winters/midsummer nights have an effect on your soul and design? Sometimes you suit your design to season (ex. Vårsalongen/Liljevalchs, a bright green floral poster in the middle of the swedish winter). What influence have traditional folkloristic art and pop art on your work? Great. What would you do if you were not a designer? Paul would be a chef and Eva a house-wife. Do you feel, there is a Scandinavian (design) identity or special approach? Yes. What are your inspirations, aims, dreams and what's your philosophy? We try to "reduce and surprice" Although this is our motto, its hard to achieve. With "reduce"

we mean that we try to say only one thing at a time.This is often the hardest part since most clients want to add as much info as possible in given space."Surprise" means we try to do the unexpected. This is also difficult as clients often expects you to do what you have already done before.

FINN HALLIN

artworks on page: 050/051 Logos, 142/143 ?! - photos
home country: Sweden • living/working in Stockholm, Sweden
email: finn.hallin@konstfack.se
date of birth: 1978
CV / short company history/ studies/ education: I have a bachelor at Konstfack Graphic Design & Illustration. Going for the master.
latest personal / commercial projects:My bachelor project: a 2 min long djungle animation. Sleeve for the EP: Idiot Savant by Chords
Do the landscapes/dark winters/midsummer nights have an effect on your soul and design? The dark winters probably made me work more. What influence have traditional folkloristic art and pop art on your work? I dont know. I try to get inspired from everywhere, so I guess I got some from pop art and folkloristic art as well. What would you do if you were not a designer? I would live a totally different life, from the start. Do you feel, there is a Scandinavian (design) identity or special approach? Yes, I see it even more when it comes to Scandinavian Illustration. People here are trendy. A lot of people follow others. But there are some really talented people here too. What are your inspirations, aims, dreams and what's your philosophy? I want to keep doing this for the fun of it. And I hope I can keep on doing my thing without having to think too much about cash. And that people will like it.

FORTH

artworks on page: 052/054 CD covers
home country: Sweden • living/working in Copenhagen, Denmark
email: mikael@forth.dk • url: www.forth.dk
date of birth / date of foundation: 06/11/28 I 01/01/01
CV / short company history/ studies/ education: studies in painting in Lund, Sweden (1 year); studies in media science in Lund and Malmö, Sweden (2 years); master's degree in design at Denmark's school of design, Copenhagen, Denmark (5 years)
latest personal / commercial projects: I'm making a t-shirt collection together with designer Anna Taws
Do the landscapes/dark winters/midsummer nights have an effect on your soul and design? Like everyone else up here, the dark winters make me really sick. I hate it. You won't get used to it either. Every year, it's a little bit worse. The spring and summertime, on the other hand, almost makes it worthwhile. The favourite is the long evenings, when the daylight very slowly transcends into darkness. Not like down south, where it gets dark just like that. What influence have traditional folkloristic art and pop art on your work? Folklore...not very much... perhaps knitting and stuff like that. Pop art.. ...guess I can't avoid being influenced by pop art. What would you do if you were not a designer? ...a truckdriver? Do you feel, there is a Scandinavian (design) identity or special approach? Scandinavian designers are quite trend-sensitive and there's often a component of irony in their work. There's a lot of comments and references to other times, other trends, other cultures. More than in other parts of Europe. Scandinavian design is quite significant, but also very homogenous, I think. What are your inspirations, aims, dreams and what's your philosophy? My greatest source of inspiration is probably my childhood. I'm brainwashed by the boxes with plastic soldiers, the petrol stations and the wallpapers of the early seventies. My aim and philosophy is to be able to do very various kinds of nice work with various people I like.

FRANS CARLQVIST

artworks on page: 140 Illustrations, 141 CD cover
home country: Sweden • living/working in Stockholm, Sweden
fax:+46 8 6699359 • email: frans@brilliant.nu • url: www.brilliant.nu/frans.html
date of birth: 15/08/1972
CV / short company history/ studies/ education: graphic design & Illustration konstfack / stockholm, freelance since 2000
latest personal / commercial projects: Label design for independent recordlabel "von"
Do the landscapes/dark winters/midsummer nights have an effect on your soul and design? Yes. What influence have traditional folkloristic art and pop art on your work? About 5%. What would you do if you were not a designer? Probably some other artform. Do you feel, there is a Scandinavian (design) identity or special approach? It might be, but it's the other stuff thats interesting. What are your inspirations, aims, dreams and what's your philosophy? To do better?

GODDUR

Gudmundur Oddur Magnusson
artworks on page: 003/005 posters, 006/007 posters - original pencil drawing by Bjarni H. Thorarinsson, 114 CD booklets, 115 Poster
home country: Iceland • living/working in Reykjavik, Iceland
fax: +354 562 3629 • email: goddur@lhi.is
date of birth: 05/06/1955
CV / short company history/ studies/ education: studied > 1986-1989 Emily Carr College of Art & Design, Vancouver, British Columbia, Canada Graphic Design (graduated with honors); 1976- 1980 Icelandic College of Art & Crafts, Reykjavik, instructors in mixed media a.o. Fluxus artists; Dieter Roth, Hermann Nitsch, Robert Filliou. (Concert tour and publication of 6LP´s "Iceland Symphony - in ten movements" with Hermann Nitsch and Dieter Roth in autumn 1981); Practice > 2002- Professor in Graphic design – Iceland Academy of the Arts; 1999-2002 Director of Studies - Iceland Academy of the Arts, 1995-1999 Head of Department - Icelandic College of Art & Crafts; 1991-1992 Graphic designer in Akureyri N-Iceland; 1989-1991 Graphic designer at ION design in Vancouver B.C.; 1981-1984 Co-founder and director - The Red House Gallery, Akureyri, Iceland; since 1992 Instructor in graphic design and free-lance graphic designer; since 1980 writer and curator on various design and fine art exhibitions
Client list includes: Reykjavik Jazz Festival, Reykjavik Art Museum, The Living Art Museum, Akureyri Art Museum, Icelandic Parliament, Badtaste Record Company, University of Iceland, Icelandic Political Science Association, Iceland Genomics Corporation, Akureyri Summer Art Festival, Iceland Art Academy, Iceland Art Festival, Kitchen Motors rec. company.
latest personal / commercial projects: Film poster for THE SEA by Baltasar Kormakur
Do the landscapes/dark winters/midsummer nights have an effect on your soul and design? Yes, but I was unaware of this until I left Iceland for studies in Vancouver, Canada. My class-mates came from different places on the globe; from Europe, East Asia, Africa and South America – For me it became obvious that my senses in terms of contrasts and moods had been activated differently - and like mine theirs where unlike mine. We felt multi-cultural, but that's very Canadian anyway - you know – Thai-Chinese Canadian style Scandinavian Smorgasbord. What influence have traditional folkloristic art and pop art on your work? As Archetypes Folkloristic art is charged with emotions which I'm aware of and I feel the presence of. Someone would put it - work autonomously from the unconscious. Your question hooks folkloristic art up with POP art - I find that interesting – I detect a pattern there! Andy working autonomously from the unconscious – ehh! What would you do if you were not a designer? A priest or a monk – No question! Do you feel, there is a Scandinavian (design) identity or special approach? I wonder when I see intellectuals of the world driving Volvos safely, communicating with their Nokia or Ericsson cellular phones - watching films - in their IKEA light wood furniture with leave patterns – about social realistic depressive child abuse in a deep Norwegian fjord or OK maybe some ABBA documentary– Yes, I feel there is a Scandinavian (design) identity with a global effect. What are your inspirations, aims, dreams and what's your philosophy? Well this not easy to sum-up – but it is simply inspiring to be here on this island and to go abroad once in awhile to feel it. Aims are something which are best forgotten and all my philosophical experiments are about doing things resulting in high-on-life here and now.

GREYSCALENET

artworks on page: 057 Image, 065 Web site »Greyscale« - 2 screens
home country: Sweden • living/working in London, England
date of foundation: 1999
url: www.greyscale.net
commercial projects: visit www.hi-res.net

GUNNAR THOR VILHJALMSSON

artworks on page: 050/051 T-Shirt I Logo, 122/123 CD booklet, 136/137 Posters, 145 Image »Krossfesting«
home country: Iceland • living/working in Reykjavik, Iceland
email: gunnar@deluxe.is • url: iwannasurfnaked.net, deluxe.is
date of birth: 08/08/1978
studies/ education: student at the Icelandic Academy of the Arts
Do the landscapes/dark winters/midsummer nights have an effect on your soul and design? Melloncollie in the wintertime, optimistic in the summertime. What influence have traditional folkloristic art and pop art on your work? They are in the mix. What would you do if you were not a designer? Olive farmer, hitman or a pro surfer. Do you feel, there is a Scandinavian (design) identity or special approach? Yes I think there is, yet sometimes it feels like special identities are slowly fading away all over the world. What are your inspirations, aims, dreams and what's your philosophy? I dream of a pineapple free world.

HÅKON KORNSTAD

artworks on page: 024/025 CD booklet, 054/055 CD covers
home country: Norway• living/working in Oslo, Norway
fax: +47 22805319 • email: hakonko@online.no • url: http://www.kornstad.com
date of birth: 05/04/1977
CV / short company history/ studies/ education: 1998-: Graphic designer, mainly for musical projects. 1998-: Professional musician. Main musical projects: Kornstad Trio, Wibutee (http://www.wibutee.net) and Bugge Wesseltoft's New Conception of Jazz. 1996-98: Jazz Studies at Music Conservatory in Trondheim
latest personal / commercial projects: Håkon Kornstad Trio: "Space Available", Music and CD sleeve
Do the landscapes/dark winters/midsummer nights have an effect on your soul and design? Perhaps the weather and landscapes up here feed me with my contrast thinking... Usually, Norwegian music has been related to an ambient, crystal-clear new age thing, but new things are happening on the scene now. The same thing can be said about design. Norwegian music and design has become more energetic and free than ever, - more Norwegian I would say. What influence have traditional folkloristic art and pop art on your work? When I did the Mari Boine Remixed cover, I searched through a pile of books about the samic clothing tradition, however later in the process I decided to use my own pictures. Overall, I'm more inspired from Warhol than vikings, I guess. What would you do if you were not a designer? Right now I'm 100% musician and 100% designer, so I guess I would be 200% musician! Do you feel, there is a Scandinavian (design) identity or special approach? I feel that the Scandinavian design tradition is more of a Swedish and Danish thing really - the Norwegians haven't contributed a lot internationally speaking. When I hear the word modern Scandinavian design I think of sober, swedish, Trade Gothic-ish typefaces set thoroughly (with all the correct ligatures) by old typographers. What are your inspirations, aims, dreams and what's your philosophy? I'm often cross-breeding between music and design: I could be on tour with a band for two weeks, then I take photos and scribble down things. When I'm home and there's an anticlimax before the next tour or musical project, I would be nailed to my mac with design things. My aim is to keep it that way and still develop both as designer and musician. Like on Wibutee's "Eight Domestic Challenges", where I was mixing the album and making the cover at the same time, - that was a dream situation for me.

HANNE CASSIM

artworks on page: 074 »Bully«, 166 Poster
home country: Denmark • living/working in Frederiksberg, Denmark
email: hanne_cassim@hotmail.com • url: www.hannecassim.dk
date of birth: 07/11/73
CV / short company history/ studies/ education: 1994-1995 / Århus Kunstakadami, Denmark; 1995-1996 / Byhøjskolens Kunstskole, Århus, Denmark; 1996-2001 / Designskolen Kolding, Department of Visual Communication, Denmark; 1999-2000 / Visiting student, Glasgow School of Art, Department of Visual Communication, Scotland; 2001- 2002 / Freelance graphic designer and illustrator: Magazine layout, illustration, Book layout, Brochures, Graphic Identities
latest personal / commercial projects: A book for a newborn baby. It contains small "pockets" where you can put al sorts of memories in. A children's book (illustration and layout) about sorrow, a project by a Danish cancer organization.
Do the landscapes/dark winters/midsummer nights have an effect on your soul and design? Nature in itself has a deep impact on me and how I feel, and in that way it has an indirect influence on my work. But a rainy day, and a bad mood can also produce very creative results. What influence have traditional folkloristic art and pop art on your work? I'm particularly inspired by pop art; it's irony, plainness and interpretation of society. It has taught me to be inspired by images in everyday life, and to dare the "simple" things. What would you do if you were not a designer? I would be a full time collector of strange and storytelling items. Or join a band? Do you feel, there is a Scandinavian (design) identity or special approach? I believe Scandinavians has a common predilection for coolness and simplicity....and I sometimes wish the Danes would be more daring in their graphic designs.... What are your inspirations, aims, dreams and what's your philosophy? I'm inspired by faces, books, magazines, packings, things found at the flea market andindeed by other graphic designers and illustrators. My dream is to continue being happy when working. My philosophy?...make the most of the photocopier, it's a wonderful tool.

JAN OKSBØL CALLESEN / GULSTUE

artworks on page: 180-183 Illustrations »Lovefighters« 180/181 Illustrations »Afrika«
home country: Denmark • living/working in Frederiksberg, Denmark
email: jan@gulstue.com • url: www.jancallesen.dk
date of birth: 27/11/73
CV / short company history/ studies/ education: I graduated from The Danish Designschool in the summer 2000, been working freelance ever since.
latest personal / commercial projects: illustrated enterpretation of Herman Bangs "Les quatre diables" and and drawing of the anatomy of the rectum for the Stop Aids Movement in Cph.
Do the landscapes/dark winters/midsummer nights have an effect on your soul and design? Everything I do has a certain sentimentality to it. It may come from the weather. What influence have traditional folkloristic art and pop art on your work? I like the strong imagery of both. What would you do if you were not a designer? I would be a sports star. Do you feel, there is a Scandinavian (design) identity or special approach? I think there is a multiplicity of sincere approaches. What are your inspirations, aims, dreams and what's your philosophy? I believe that pictures can articulate what can´t be conceived intellectually. You get smarter making pictures. Even watching pictures can make you brighter. It´s all about perception.

JOHN J. CANDY DESIGN

John Esberg & David Kandell
artworks on page: 128 CD cover, 137 Poster I Illustration
home country: Sweden • living/working in Stockholm, Sweden
email: bigboss@johnjcandy.com • url: www.johnjcandy.com
date of birth: John "ACE" Esberg -71 & David "SANDY" Kandell-73
date of foundation: May 99
Studies & Education: Beckmans School of Design/Graphic design & Commercial Art. (Bachelor Degree); CV: John & David has worked on advertising agencies in Stockholm.
Latest personal projects: Monday Bar Techno Experience CD / Latest commercial projects: JC Jeans & Clothes, Axel & Margaret Ax:son Johnson Foundation
Do the landscapes/dark winters/midsummer nights have an effect on your soul and design? Dark winters and midsummer nights have an enormous effect on our soul and senses. Beautiful landscapes, divine Swedish mother nature, landslide and archipelago have a "hocus-pocus" impact on our emotions. No matter what time of the year, even through harsh climate periods when your feeling like half a man, nature is top recreation. Works as soulfood and refreshment to our minds. The colouring in our works, tend to be "full on" or "sparkling". Our graphics tend to communicate a kind of "energy" or "temperament", that we truly believe, sweet mother earth is reminding us of her mighty grace. Working climate is much more harsh. The real darkness and cold effects are the stress of information overdose, cold turkey design, "impotent" burned-out small market and overheated ears because of soppy bollocks. What influence have traditional folkloristic art and pop art on your work? None, in particular influence in our design, but our work often describe signals that are relevant to the case. A certain relevant reason. It tells a story, and the consumer gets a direct idea. But stretched tight clothing on tall blondes, that are stomping along in clogs, sure put a big smile across our faces. As we all know Sweden is sexually open minded, including us. What would you do if you were not a designer? David: Diver or a dolphin. John: Sailor or a fox. Do you feel, there is a Scandinavian (design) identity or special approach? For us typical Scandinavian design is clean, minimalistic, distinct, correct, functional and very asexual. What are your inspirations, aims, dreams and what's your philosophy? Inspirations? It's lays in the urbanism and all that comes and goes with it. Living in layers of difference. Nice mantra and karma. Aims? To be unconditional, artistic, loving, conscios and awake. To create solutions that makes people think. It's not illegal yet. Colour the world. Dreams? We're dreaming of total harmony, peace, freedom and simple life underneath the sun. Philosophy? "WE COME IN PEACE"

JONAS BANKER / BANKERWESSEL

artworks on page: 204/205 CD Covers I Illustrations
home country: Sweden • living/working in Stockholm, Sweden
fax: +46.8.411.17.63 • email: jonas@bankerwessel.com • www.bankerwessel.com
date of birth / date of foundation: 1968 I 2002
latest personal / commercial projects: Konstfack, University College of arts crafts and design '91-'97, Otis College of art and design, Los Angeles '95-'96, I've been working as a freelancer up until 2002 when I started a design company together with Ida Wessel. Right now I'm finishing up a project for the Fifa world cup site.
Do the landscapes/dark winters/midsummer nights have an effect on your soul and design? I think there's a certain gloomy Nordic mood to my work, hopefully there are more sides there as well. I always find the best work to be a clash between two opposite feelings. What influence have traditional folkloristic art and pop art on your work? I've always enjoyed the naivistic aspect of folkloristic art. American pop art from the sixties has been a major influence. Even if I tend to be influenced by a lot of different things I always go back to the pop era. What would you do if you were not a designer? I really don't know. When you focus so hard on one thing it's really difficult to imagine doing something else. I like feta cheese, perhaps I could be a feta cheese maker. Do you feel, there is a Scandinavian (design) identity or special approach? Yes, definitely, there's a strong Scandinavian identity. A will to explain and to be understood, that everything is there for reason. Not to decorate and to be arbitrary. Sometimes I'm very happy to be a part of all that and sometimes I have a strong need to get away from it. What are your inspirations, aims, dreams and what's your philosophy? My inspiration differs all the time, could be anything really, buildings, shoes or birds. At the moment though, I have a thing for Jean-Paul Goude/ Grace Jones and Ettore Sottsass/Memphis. My aim is always to do better stuff and I hope that it is still understandable and enjoyable in ten years time. My philosophy is to be true to oneself and enjoy life.

KALIBER10000 / K10K

artworks on page: 062/063 Web site »Moodstats« - screens I Web site »k10k« - screens I Poster
home country: Denmark, UK, USA • living/working in San Francisco, USA
email: m@k10k.net, toke@k10k.net • url: www.k10k.net
date of foundation:1998
CV / short company history/ studies/ education: Michael Schmidt and Toke Nygaard are a pair of award-winning Danish designers, web developers and all-around sauerkraut munchers. They are the founders of Kaliber10000™ [http://www.k10k.net], one of the world's largest design portals, and their works have been featured in magazines, books and periodicals from Hong Kong to Malmö. Together with technical wizard Per Jørgensen they are also the creators of Moodstats™ - an innovative piece of emotional software which allows the users to record, rate and analyze their moods on a day-to-day basis. They are currently based in London & San Francisco, and spend their days doing designy things, fiddling around with unfinished personal projects and trying not to get too heavily involved with 'The Man'.
latest personal / commercial projects: Moodstats, www.moodstats.net
Do the landscapes/dark winters/midsummer nights have an effect on your soul and design? Yes, indeed. That is why Michael and Toke have sought refuge in sunny California. What influence have traditional folkloristic art and pop art on your work? Not much I would say. I guess you are affected by the influenced that have run through you growing up in scandinavia, but our work is not particularly based on any region specific influences. What would you do if you were not a designer? Toke a musician. Michael a print designer. Per an inventor of time machines and spaceships. Do you feel, there is a Scandinavian (design) identity or special approach? I would say that Nordic design has a certain feel to it, some of the time. Like you would sometimes be able to pick out a piece of work and say "this is Japanese".. But when dealing with web graphics I find that much design is very 'hybrid', people get very inspired by different things with no local connection. What are your inspirations, aims, dreams and what's your philosophy? We simply want to fill a gap; we aim to produce the kinds of sites and software that we want to use, but do not exist out there. All our products have been born out of this need for something that either wasn't there or wasn't good enough.

KARLSSONWILKER INC.

artworks on page: 011 CD images, 054 CD cover, 131 CD cover I Poster
home country: Iceland, US of A, etc. • living/working in New York City, US of A
fax: +1 212 929 8063 • email: tellmewhy@karlssonwilker.com • url: www.karlssonwilker.com
date of foundation: late 2000
CV / short company history/ studies/ education: karlssonwilker inc. is the new york based design company of Hjalti Karlsson and Jan Wilker. The Icelander Hjalti, who worked with Stefan Sagmeister for four years before starting his own enterprise with his friend Jan, recieved his BFA from parsons school of design, ny. Jan graduated from the state academy of fine art stuttgart, germany. In their Manhattan studio four people work on various projects, ranging from restaurant to book designs, from music to cosmetic packaging, from moving images to interactive and product design, blablabla. Both were ADC Young Guns in 2001.clients include: Warner Bros., Virgin, Capitol, VH1, USAcable, Anne Klein New York, Dreamworks, Universal, Sharksucker Surfgear, Princeton Architectural Press, Goldman Properties, Diesel, Worldstudio Foundation,... > From time to time, there are parties on their little backyard rooftop.
latest personal / commercial projects: Hjalti: going to the gym more often / designing a book, Jan: improving his kissing / doing stuff for a rock band
Do the landscapes/dark winters/midsummer nights have an effect on your soul and design? They defenitely would play an active role in our overall feel, if we would be located in Iceland. but we're not. What influence have traditional folkloristic art and pop art on your work? As much as everything else. What would you do if you were not a designer? Hjalti:

candy salesman. Jan: the same. Do you feel, there is a Scandinavian (design) identity or special approach? Yes, but it's not that visible anymore; it looks like design was one of the first things affected by globalisation. What are your inspirations, aims, dreams and what's your philosophy? We try to love everything what we do and to have fun with all this.

KATRIN PETURSDOTTIR / MY STUDIO LTD.

artworks on page: 178 Illustration »In The Woods«, 179 Illustration »Ribbons«
home country: Iceland • living/working in Reykjavik, Iceland
fax: +354 561 2315 • email: katrin.petursd@lhi.is, katrin@simnet.is
date of birth / date of foundation: 11/02/67 I march 2000
CV / short company history/ studies/ education: 1990, Foundation Course, Polycrea, Paris, 1990-1995, Design diploma, Industrial Design, E.S.D.I Paris, 1996, Product development, Philippe Starck, Paris, 1997, Product development, Ross Lovegrove, London. 1998-2002, Product development, Michael Young, MY Studio ltd, Reykjavik. 2000-2002, Director of Studies, Iceland Art Academy, Iceland
latest personal / commercial projects: Illustrations and graphics for Michael Young as the guest of honour at INTERIEUR, Belgium.Illustration for BHV Christmas window, Paris.
Do the landscapes/dark winters/midsummer nights have an effect on your Soul and design? Definitely, it is impossible to live with the extremes of darkness for months and then constant light without being influenced by it. It kind of drives you crazy...in good ways and bad ways. What influence have traditional folkloristic art and pop art on your work? Iceland has never been very strong in the department of folkloristic art, the reason for this is an association of hostility of life, at least in the past and lack of materials to work with. However, one might say that a folkloristic spirit hovers around and always has in the form of stories and ideas of ideal dimensions which supposedly coexist with our world. This can be very inspiring in a private sort of way but generally people travel quite a lot these days so it´s difficult to speak of one source of inspiration. What would you do if you were not a designer? I have no idea, probably fine art. Do you feel, there is a Scandinavian (design) identity or special approach? There is a design heritage in the other Scandinavian countries and a sense of scandinavianess in the Nordic countries which I belief has trapped many designers creatively over the years. I don't believe national identity goals make much sense today and I think many people are seeing themselves as part of a larger community. What are your inspirations, aims, dreams and what's your philosophy? When I studied Industrial Design in Paris, I found myself constantly burying my nose in books on plants, animals and biological structures. At that time I didn´t see much point in it but was totally fascinated by all the stuff never the less. When I started working with computer technology I felt the urge to explore and create catalogues of symbols which I would use in a calculated way to create imaginary worlds. What interests me in this is how the symbols can develop their own kinetic momentum with in a structure that I create for them through repetition. Currently I´m exploring ways to animate these worlds. My goal is to continue to cultivate my private space and work towards freedom.

KIM HIORTHØY

artworks on page: 075 CD cover, 157-160 Record sleeves, 161 Poster, 162 CD cover, 164 Illustration, 165 CD covers
home country: Norway • living/working in Oslo, Norway
fax: +47 22 80 01 00 • email: kimim@online.no
url: www.runegrammofon.com / www.smalltownsupersound.com
date of birth: 1973
CV / short company history/ studies/ education: Trondheim Academy of Fine Art, Trondheim 1991-1996, School of Visual Arts, NYC 1994-1995 Royal Academy of Fine Art, Copenhagen 1998-2000
latest personal / commercial projects: ep for Chemical Underground, rune grammofon book
Do the landscapes/dark winters/midsummer nights have an effect on your soul and design? Yes. What influence have traditional folkloristic art and pop art on your work? 50% What would you do if you were not a designer? Sing. Do you feel, there is a Scandinavian (design) identity or special approach? No. What are your inspirations, aims, dreams and what's your philosophy? To thicken the plot.

KINGSIZE

artworks on page: 137 Poster
home country: Sweden • living/working in Stockholm, Sweden.
fax: +46 8 702 14 68 • email:mika@kingsizegraphics.com / andreas@kingsizegraphics.com
url:www.kingsizegraphics.com
date of foundation: 1998
CV / short company history/ studies/ education: Mika Pollack: Beckmans School of design (3 years), employed at Acne International. Andreas Pettersson: Beckmans School of design (3 years), employed at Arnek.
latest personal / commercial projects: Illustrations and design for Swedish IRS in collaboration with TBWA sthlm. Illustrations for company/service. Smart meeting, in collaboration with Blond Swedish Amateurs.
Do the landscapes/dark winters/midsummer nights have an effect on your soul and design? The Swedish winter is good for working but bad for the soul. What influence have traditional folkloristic art and pop art on your work? Pop art some, folklore none. What would you do if you were not a designer? Mika: A producer / musician or wrestler. Andreas: Special effects artist or Ice hockey professional. Do you feel, there is a Scandinavian (design) identity or special approach? Maybe, and if so we feel it has changed from the traditional minimalistic to something more diverse. What are your inspirations, aims, dreams and what's your philosophy? Inspiration: music, books, movies, computer games. Aims: World domination. Dreams: Titanium Powerbook 800 mhz + Motu 828. Philosophy: DE eVOlution

KJEKS

Lill-Hege Klausen
artworks on page: 195 Illustration »Mountain«
home country: Norway • living/working in Oslo, Norway
fax: +47 22 38 00 41 • email: lill-hege@kjeks.nu • url: www.kjeks.nu
date of birth / date of foundation: 12.10.74 / established KJEKS together with my sister in May 1999
CV / short company history/ studies/ education:I founded KJEKS in May 1999 together with my sister (Nina Klausen) as I wanted to focus on illustrations and move a bit away from graphic design. In January 2001 Torgeir Holm, a graphic designer, illustrator and animator joined us. And in November 2001 Viktor Grindheim joined us. In January 2002 we also got a copy writer, Ole-Henrik Larsen on our team. The company is a creative cooperative were everyone is a equal.
latest personal / commercial projects: In January 2002 KJEKS Norsk Forms annual price for graphic design. (Its a annual price were one industrial designer, one architect, one interior designer, one kunsthåndtverker and a graphic designer reiceives a "young ang promising" price for beeing "particulary talented, stimulating and convincing in their work"). In connection with the price we had a exibition at the gallery Norsk Form
Do the landscapes/dark winters/midsummer nights have an effect on your soul and design? I come from the north of Norway. Were the landscape is rather rough. High mountains way down into the ocean. The clima is tough, and the weather changes quickly. In the summertime it´s light all day and night. In the winter there is a long period when you never get to see daylight, and it feels like everything is snow and darkness. I do belive this effects peoples soul, but can you see it in my work - I really don´t know... What influence have traditional folkloristic art and pop art on your work? None that I an aware of actually. Though I must say that I like pop-art. I find it to be amusing and entertaining. I like that fact that it´s playful and not to "serious" if you know what I mean. Too many things are... What would you do if you were not a designer? Ha - good question. I really dont know. When I say I really don´t know it´s because there is so many interesting, funny and good ways of spending my time. But if we say that lack of interrest is the only restriction I would love to work with fabrics. Making fabrics or choosing fabrics for furniture, clothes etc.. Writing would be wonderful. Not poetry, but novels. I get great pleasure from animal, plants and flowers - so gardening maybe? Taking care of a large garden or a park. A vet perhaps? Althoug I know I would have a huge problem if someone wantet to put their cat to sleep.(I would probably end up with a home filled with animals... not a good idea really....) . Well - I could go on. It´s so many interesting things one can do. It´s easier to say what I don´t want to do :) Do you feel, there is a Scandinavian (design) identity or special approach? Hm - I suppose there is.The first word that pos out is simplicity. I suppose this "simplicity" is a bit typical for scandinavia in general - though I know there are people that would strongly disagree with me on this :) When I get comments on my work it´s guite often regarding things like my use of colors an the overall expression. Eventhoug I do different type of styles, it seems like I always keep a "simple, cold and clean" feeling/expression and a certain distance. What are your inspirations, aims, dreams and what's your philosophy? My philosophy is guite simple - do what you enjoy and enjoy what you do. My work is not important like the the work of say a doctor. This means that is even more important that you enjoy your work. Cause really - you can´t look back and say that " So, I worked my ass of, but hey I did meet all my deadlines". When people talk about the pressure in this kind of work - I do know what they mean, but I strongly suggest that they take a step back and have a look at what they actually work with. We don´tsave people. We don´t change the world. We don´t fight for what we belive in. What you´re left with is the chance to play and have fun so really; don´t take your self to seriosly. That way you´ll have a good time, and I also belive that´s when you´ll do you´re best work :) Inspiration. It can be a person you see in the street, the light on a quite ordinary day, music you hear from a cafe or the sounds from an open window. I find inspiration in everything. The only challenge is to "be there" when you´re really there and not trouble your mind with all kinds of worries, pressure and disturbing thoughts. At times it might be difficult, but when you succeed it truly worth it!

KVAD

Kjetil Vatne
artworks on page: 206 Illustration, 208/209 Illustrations, 211 Illustrations
home country: Norway • living/working in Bergen, Norway
email: vatne@online.no • url: http://www.kvad.com <http://www.kvad.com/>
date of birth / date of foundation: 07.07.76 I ca. 1995
CV / short company history/ studies/ education: been working freelance for national and international clients. Doing design work for web, print, clothing, stores, profiles, GUIs, 3D etc. as well as personal projects.
latest personal / commercial projects: personal: kvad.v6/flowing patterns (RIGHTnow) commercial: Soria Moria/patterns for childrens sweaters and jackets
Do the landscapes/dark winters/midsummer nights have an effect on your soul and design? The difference in daylight between winter and summer certainly has an effect. It's very hard to avoid the winter depressions when it's dark almost all the time. On the other hand winter is also the most productive part of the year. Unlike summer just going out and enjoying yourself in the sun isn't much of an option. You have to actively do something to keep your mood up. In the summer when it's warm and nice weather I prefer to just sit outside in the sun. Recharge my batteries for the oncoming winter. What influence have traditional folkloristic art and pop art on your work? Neither folkloristic nor pop art are an active source of irtspiration for me. But as everyone else I'm a product of the society I live in, so I probably do pick up inspiration from those parts as well, I just don't do it consciously. What would you do if you were not a designer? I'm quiet certain it would have to be something visually oriented as well. Wether I define myself as a designer, artist or whatever isn't that important, it's all something that floats into each other. I do have a strong wish to be able to cut down on the commercial projects and do more of my own work. Working more together with other artists wether that be musicians, actors, painters etc where we could merge our different viewpoints into something new. I haven't really explored other options outside of the visual realm. Since I was 2 years old my interests have always been visually oriented in different ways. Do you feel, there is a Scandinavian (design) identity or special approach? To a certain extent there seems to be. I do feel there is less of a common identity here in Norway than there is in i.e. Sweden. Seems a bit more chaotic here. I think that's a good thing. The more variety the better. But then again, I'm not able to observe this from the outside. So perhaps to someone from the outside the common identity between the Scandinavian countries are obvious. I've never tied my identity to being Norwegian or Scandinavian though. Just myself. What are your inspirations, aims, dreams and what's your philosophy? Inspiration can come from anywhere, wether it's an old couple sitting at a bus stop, some object or color combination or a mood swing. From there on things often mutate into something else, the original inspiration is usually just a starting point. I'm always searching, observing, but without any definite aim. They appear in small flashes, - creating something I'm satisfied with, - getting reactions from other people etc. I always have to push myself ahead, very few things ever come for free. I hope never to stagnate in evolving myself (both workwise and personally). Never to find "my expression" and stick with it. The expression in my work usually evolves in cycles. I can do a certain kind of work for maybe half a year, and when I've done that I search for something new. I just reach a natural point when I'm done with it. Doing the same thing over and over seems pointless to me. Most of my work are very much driven ahead by aesthetics and moods. The ones I'm the most fond of myself are the ones that are deeply personal to me, linked in some way to events in my life. I don't have a need to communicate the stories behind those feelings/moods, just the moods themselves. At first glance to someone else I don't think the difference is all that obvious. But then again that's what I think is great about it, every ones personal experience will be different, and theirs is no less worth than what my experience is. There is no right or wrong interpretation. The works I've created that are purely aesthetic are much more hollow to me. They just merge with the background. Meaningless apart from perhaps being "cool". Colors, simplicity and silence have been very important to me through all my life. To capture drama through that. Making pictures can sometimes work as therapy for me, one of the few places I'm able to escape into another world.

LOTTA KÜHLHORN

artworks on page: 037 »Rosemarys Baby«, 149 »Die Liebe ist kälter als Tod«, 152 »Ice-Storm«, 153 »Taxi driver - Dress« I »Snow-White« I »Allt Om Min Mamma«, 154 »2001 A«, 155 »2001 B«, 156 »The Party«
home country: Sweden • living/working in Stockholm, Sweden
fax: +46 8 643 85 08 • email: lotta@kuhlhorn.se
date of birth: 29/07/63
CV / short company history/ studies/ education: Konstfack 83 - 87, freelance designer and Illustrator since then
latest personal / commercial projects: growing corn/ making patterns for IKEA/ designing bookcovers
Do the landscapes/dark winters/midsummer nights have an effect on your soul and design? Soul: yes, Design: maybe, maybe not. What influence have traditional folkloristic art and pop art on your work? 100% What would you do if you were not a designer? Criminal investigator. Do you feel, there is a Scandinavian (design) identity or special approach? Yes. What are your inspirations, aims, dreams and what's your philosophy? Inspiration: things that surrounds me philosophy: "I am for an art" (Claes Oldenburg)

MAI-BRITT AMSLER

artworks on page: 075 CD cover, 078/079 Illustrations »Create Your Job« I »Who Are You?« I »Stress« I »The Silent Man«, 133 Illustrations I CD cover, 190 »Europa«
home country: Denmark • living/working in Copenhagen, Denmark
email: mail@maibrittamsler.dk / maiamsler@hotmail.com • url: www.maibrittamsler.dk
date of birth: 23/04/1973
CV / short company history/ studies/ education: 1995 - 2000: Danmarks Designskole, Copenhagen; 1999: Hochschule für Gestaltung und Kunst, Zürich; 2001-: works as a grafic designer / illustrator
latest personal / commercial projects: Identity / logo for Copenhagen X, Urban and Housing Exhibition
Do the landscapes/dark winters/midsummer nights have an effect on your soul and design? Yes, in that way that I get more work done in the winter when it is nice and cosy to be inside. What influence have traditional folkloristic art and pop art on your work? I think popart has an influence on most grafic designers because of the mixture of art and mass-communication. What would you do if you were not a designer? Be a writer. Do you feel, there is a Scandinavian (design) identity or special approach? If there is, I think people outside of Scandinavia can see it more clearly than the scandinavians. What are your inspirations, aims, dreams and what's your philosophy? To work by intuition in combination with strategy. Working without noticing time, to have fun with what I do and to make a living.

MADS BERG / GULSTUE

artworks on page: 192/193 Illustrations
home country: Denmark • living/working in Copenhagen, Denmark
email: mads@gulstue.com • url: www.,madsberg.com / www.gulstue.com
date of birth: 1975
CV / short company history/ studies/ education: graduated from Danish Designschool 2000, company Mads Berg founded same year, various illustration-jobs thereafter.
latest personal / commercial projects: Commercial: artwork, characterdesign for the Motorola youth campaign HelloMoto / PartyMoto 2002 in 14 countries. Personal: The childrens book "A day at the Tiny Island"
Do the landscapes/dark winters/midsummer nights have an effect on your soul and design? Often in the dark winter months, I find myself happily preoccupied with work, since there is not much worth staying outdoor for. What influence have traditional folkloristic art and pop art on your work? Popart made graphics legal in fine art, which is fine. Folkloristic and primitive folk art is not to be considered art, but a fine means of communication between everybody. The simpleness of this can be inspirational. Mostly I am inspired by patterns and the element of repetition in folkloristic art. What would you do if you were not a designer? I would probably be sheep, or a cartographer. Do you feel, there is a Scandinavian (design) identity or special approach? The remoteness of Scandinavia to central Europe might cause a stressed sense of 'having to live up to' and 'got to be hip'. This stress is a special, accelarated approach. And, some design ideas might emerge from a serious alcoholic intake, thus, more fanstastic. What are your inspirations, aims, dreams and what's your philosophy? Good workmanship, silly ideas, intelligent reflection, fun in the making.

MILES + MARVIN

artworks on page: 020/021
home country: Norway
Who knows these guys?

MISSION DESIGN AGENCY

Nicolai Schaanning Larsen
artworks on page: 016/017 Selfpromotion »Mission« - cards, 018 Selfpromotion, 022 Selfpromotion »Mission« - card, 032 CD cover »Oyster«, 032/033/034/035 Experimental T-shirt design for DieselStyleLab - Catalogue + cards, 121 Image for poster
home country: Norway • living/working in Oslo, Norway
fax: +47 2411 0501 • email: nicolai@mission.no • url: www.mission.no
date of birth / date of foundation: 09/08/1976 / Mission founded 2001
CV / short company history/ studies/ education: 1999- 2001 BA Honours Graphic design Central St. Martins College of art and Design (CSM) London, England. 1998- 1999 BA Honours in Graphic design and Media, London College of Printing (LCP) London, England. 1997-1998 Mac Design,Merkantilt institute, Oslo, Norway. Work experience: 2001 Mission design agency, Designer. Worked for clients as Telenor, Jazid collective, Slowsupreme, easypark. 2001 Dieselstylelab: A experimetal and a new extraordinary vision that celebrates the diesel stylelab ethos, individuality, progression and orginality. This was represented by an in-store campaigne and a T-shirt collection in the London and New York store. Working also at Central St. martins degree show theme and identity program. This includes degree show invitations, posters, show catalog, cd-rom and website. Clubconcept for Mezzo, Club inteam, which included identity, flyer, poster and VIPcard. 2000 Corporate identity for OsloscopeRecords. This work included facade signage, posters, flyers, stickers, advertising and website. 2000 Corporate identity for Itel. [Inteligent telecom service as] 1998-1999 Experimental magazine by Nine design. Nine Design consisteted of designer students from LCP and CSM. Corporate identity for Telepluss [You communications]
Short company history: Mission is a design agency specialising in branding. The agency was founded in 2001 and has already attracted a good number of clients as well as recieved numerouse awards and a high creative recognition.The team is varied in skills, interests, age and nationalities, and we believe that bringing these different talents together will create inspiring solutions.
Do the landscapes/dark winters/midsummer nights have an effect on your soul and design? The winter in norway tends to be dark and cold, the suicide static increases up in north and people get depressed. So it does effect peoples mind and soul, and thats what we use as a tool to be creative. Me myself tend to digg into my own little world and play even harder... What influence have traditional folkloristic art and pop art on your work? I think alot of my studentswork where influence by norwegian folkloristic art, but it is funny that most of it was actually done in uk while I was studing there. What would you do if you were not a designer? Explorer... Do you feel, there is a Scandinavian (design) identity or special approach? I feel there was, but now that internet has become on of the most used inspiration sources, I think that it´s hard to say whats typical scandinavian design. It seems that "less is more" something scandinavian designers been trigged by, but everything seems to go in a direction of "less isn´t good enough"... What are your inspirations, aims, dreams and what's your philosophy? Me, myself and my lost world. Inspiration I get from what I see, hear and experience around me. Love is also a great inspiration, it´s like everything and nothing at the same time... Music seems to create dreams which make my mind leap away from this world, into my own...this is where I create my best work. I also love to hang out in the library were you find all kinds of stuff...especially the books that you not allowed to borrow tends to be the one with the most interesting stuff inside. Being given freedom can lead to some amazing work... I still wonder what I´m gone do in life...there are so many questions...so many thoughts...so many roads... I want to create...I want anwers...I want more love...I want freedom. One of the great things about the future is that there are no rules.

MONGREL

artworks on page: 027 CD Cover I Label, 029/030/031 Wallpaper, 048 Catalogue + packaging, 049 Poster I Packaging I Illustration, 050/051 Illustration I Logo s I Poster I Flyer, 053 Logo typeface, 060/061 Illustrations, 111 Flyers, 148 Illustrations I Typeface logo, 149 Typeface, 150/151 Patterns - Camouflage I Wallpapers, 177 Illustration
home country: Finland • living/working in Helsinki, Finland
email: info@mongrelassociates.com • url: www.mongrelassociates.com
date of foundation: August 2001
CV / short company history/ studies/ education: Studied either at Lahti Institute of Art and Design, Mongrel was set up following all having met working at Taivas Hel (formally www.hel13.com) or at Taivas Design. All part of a larger advertising agency. After all leaving and starting new jobs we became very disatisfied with the whole scene here. So we decided to do it alone.
latest personal / commercial projects: following work done for Dazed & Confused Magazine (February Issue), Junya Watanabe at Comme des Garcon will be producing 50 limited edition prints of the design made. They will be sold exclusively at Comme des Garcon, Tokyo.
Do the landscapes/dark winters/midsummer nights have an effect on your soul and design? Yes, they do. We take all these aspects and use them in our work in a new exciting way. What would you do if you were not a designer? Have never thought of anything else. It all comes naturally to do what we are doing. Do you feel, there is a Scandinavian (design)

identity or special approach? Within the arts throughout history we have been influenced by nature. That is what is Scandinavian design.

MONO CYKLON

Gytz
artworks on page: 055 Posters, 069 Image »Repair«,
home country: Denmark • living/working in Copenhagen, Denmark
email: mono@cyklon.dk • url: www.monocyklon.net
Date of birth /Date of foundation: Thursday '71 I Summer '98
CV / short company history/ studies/ education: Originally founded as Cyklon in '98 which existed on and off in different constellations. Refounded as Mono Cyklon by Gytz in '01 after a one year working period at Büro Destruct in Switzerland. [Looking for a partner at present]
Latest personal / Commercial projects: My website and typefaces/ Album cover for the weirdo-jazz musician Hess.
Do the landscapes/dark winters/midsummer nights have an effect on your soul and design? I would rather say that the sea has an effect on my soul: I feel like being in a kind of vacuum if it is not in close vicinity. Although the winters are long and depressive, I think they have a melancholic grace that inspires me. What influence has traditional folkloristic art and pop art on your work? I have always admired ornaments from the antiquity and the viking age, but I do not think you will see the influence in my work. What would you do if you were not a designer? I would probably have a university degree in history. Do you feel, there is a Scandinavian (design) identity or special approach? Simplicity. What are your inspirations, aims, dreams and what's your philosophy? My primary inspiration comes from Bauhaus, Dadaism and Constructivisme - otherwise I am inspired by the nature and life that surrounds me. I prefer not to talk about my dreams, I rather make them come true. My philosophy would be something like: Maintain a strong integrity!

NATHALIE NYSTAD

artworks on page: 132 Illustrations, 134 Illustrations, 170/171 Illustrations, 176 Illustrations
home country: Denmark • living/working in Copenhagen, Denmark
email: nn@entegrate.dk / nn@la-familia.dk
date of birth: 27/09/71
CV / short company history/ studies/ education: Danmarks Designskole, Favrica, Benetton
Do the landscapes - dark winters/midsummer nights have an effect on your soul and design? My own life reflects that changing of the seasons. I go through light and darkness. What would you do if you were not a designer? Write. Do you feel, there is a Scandinavian (design) identity or special approach? Our good sense of humour. What are your inspirations, aims, dreams and what's your philosophy? My drawings is my sholtor. I learn life through my hand. It's the best way for me to think and realize.

NINA BEIER

artworks on page: 109 Posters for an art exhibition (collaboration with Jan Callesen), 176 Illustrations
home country: Denmark • living/working in Copenhagen, Denmark
email: nina@ninabeier.dk • url: www.ninabeier.dk
date of birth: 22/12/75
CV / short company history/ studies/ education: Bachelor: Danmarks Designskole; MA: to be taken at Royal College of Art beginning September. Co-founded the Danish magazine Rart in 1999, photo/art-editor and contributor since.
latest personal / commercial projects: Music video for Danish band moi Caprice, CD cover design for Danish band moi Caprice, Mikael Simpson and Lise W. 11 photographs in the exhibition Edge in Øksnehallen, Copenhagen. Art and photo editor of Danish magazine Rart, and contributing with 2 picture series. Photo campaign for Danish fashion designer M and Paris-based designer Daniel Schou. Photography for posters, web site, postcards etc. for Danish STOP AIDS Campaign. Millenium of Mode – International Fashion Photography Festival, TokyoFashion Museum: 12 pictures in collaboration with photographer Helena Christensen
Do the landscapes - dark winters/midsummer nights have an effect on your soul and design? I can´t seem to escape the foggy tone in my pictures, so I suppose so. What would you do if you were not a designer? I wish I would make music. Do you feel, there is a Scandinavian (design) identity or special approach? I think we generally tend to work in a very driven and controlled way resulting in thought-through projects which unfortunately often lack impulsiveness and spark. What are your inspirations, aims, dreams and what's your philosophy? I am inspired by the approach that the art-world takes to expressing itself, but on the other hand I am fascinated by the massproduction of the commercial medias. I like the magazine, because of the way the picture series and fashion stories catch the viewers "off-guard". This gives new possibilities for story-telling for the commercial world as well as for the art-world. I want to tell honest personal stories, where people least expect it. I reckon the same thing is possible in music videos.

OSKAR KORSAR

artworks on page: 172/173 Record sleeves, 174/175 llustrations, 176 Illustrations
home country: Sweden • living/working in Stockholm, Sweden
fax: 46 8 54588586 • email: oskar@reala.se • url:www.t0rbj0rn.com/oskarkorsar
date of birth: 18/08/77
CV / short company history/ studies/ education: Ba on graphic design and illustration at konstfack. Having my own company since one year ago.
latest personal / commercial projects: Working on a exibition and a new comic book at the moment.
Do the landscapes/dark winters/midsummer nights have an effect on your soul and design? I think so. What influence have traditional folkloristic art and pop art on your work? I was interested in folklore in my first years at college. Now I'm just interested in fine art painting from the old masters (and the new.) And google image. But I still like it, but I'm not so much into it anymore. Maybe I have created a new folkloristic art. So maybe it was a lie. Anyway, I hate pop art. (at the moment anyway) What would you do if you were not a designer? I'm not working so much at hit designs so maybe I would be a designer. Or a painter. Or a author. But I understand that you mean something else so actually I have no idea. I have no experience in some other works. I have no dreams. Do you feel, there is a Scandinavian (design) identity or special approach? I think that if you wont to have it you can have it. But I dont care. So it's up to you. What are your inspirations, aims, dreams and what's your philosophy? To be able to create artificial worlds that effect peoples mind and bodies.

PAW NIELSEN / KONSTRUKTION

artworks on page: 058/059 CD covers
home country: Denmark • living/working in Copenhagen, Denmark
telephone: +45 26 15 28 60 (mobile)
date of birth: 08/09/1973
CV / Short history / studies / education: 1994–1999: Institute for Visual communication: Graphic Design, Designskolen Kolding, Denmark. 1999-2001: Layout for Politiken, leading danish newspaper. 2001: Graphic design for Jazz Special magazine and Stunt Records, Denmark. 2001-2002: Freelance / working at Gul Stue, Copenhagen, www.gulstue.com 2002 -: Freelance / working out of my own home.
Latest personal / commercial projects: Graphic design for Fever Pitch, american underground avant garde music magazine. Various up-coming posters and CD cover projects.
Do the landscape / dark winters / midsummer nights have any affect on your soul and design? Don't believe it has, I seek my input in music and cinema, not so much in the weather outside. What influences have traditional folkloristic art and pop art on your work? I see myself as quite internationally minded, so I'd say very little or at least none that I'm aware of. What would you do if you were not a designer? MUSIC! I'd rush out and buy a sampler and seek for the perfect beat. Do you feel there is a scandinavian (design) identity or special approach? Certainly. The scandinavian culture and also design is thought of as kinda clean and neat. That is reflected in much of the well-known designs. I see some of that cleaness in my own work, but I don't think it's necessarily very scandinavian, though. What are your inspirations, aims, dreams and what's your philosphy? Inspiration comes from music, from film, from growing up, from the process of working, and many times when you least expect it. Aims and dreams are to do work I'm proud of, not to do work I feel is void of meaning and creativity. The philosophy is to have no restrictions. And keep the design where the heart is, for things rebellious, political, aesthetical and musical.

PEHMUSTE

Aleksi Kemppainen
artworks on page: 050/051 T-Shirt, 066/067 Web site »Pehmuste« - screens, 210 Illustration
home country: Finland • living/working in Helsinki, Finland
email: leksi@pehmuste.com • url: http://www.pehmuste.com
date of birth: 10/10/1981
latest personal / commercial projects: www.pehmuste.com

PIA WALL / STAVANGERILLUSTRATØRENE

artworks on page: 053 Security symbols, 061 Poster, 194 Illustrations - Swim caps, 196-201 Illustrations - Pin up book / chapter divider
home country: I am 1/2 Swedish, 1/2 Norwegian • living/working in Stavanger, Norway
fax: + 47 51 91 68 06
email: pia@stavanger-illustratorene.no • url: www.stavanger-illustratorene.no
date of birth: 25/07/63 • foundation of Stavangerillustratørene: year 2000
CV / short company history/ studies/ education: 1992-1993. Exchange student 1 year - SHKS, (Oslo, Norway). 1994-1995. Exchange student 1, 3 year - ESAG (Paris, France), 1996. Master of Fine Art - HDK (Göteborg, Sweden). 1996-2000. Running my own studio. 2000- going: on Running a studio with Stavangerillustratørene. 2001- going on: UNA(London) Designers, working on projects with Nick Bell
latest personal / commercial projects:Layout for eye magazine (may 2002). Illustrations for SHELL´s (Norway) Annual report (April 2002).108 (!!!) icons / illustrations for Science Museum, London (March / April 2002). Layout for eye magazine (February 2002). Illustrations for Pin Up Book for Taschen, "Bernard of Hollywood" (November 2001- still going on). Creating the cover and some layout for eye magazine (August 2001)
Do the landscapes/dark winters/midsummer nights have an effect on your soul and design? Yes, I am probably effected, but I don´t know how... What influence have traditional folkloristic art and pop art on your work? I am not sure. I find inspiration in good illustrators, designers, photographers and artists like; Sara Fanelli, Benoît Godde, J.Otto Seibold, Nick Bell, Martin Parr and Takashi Murakami. What would you do if you were not a designer? I think I would like to be a photographer. I took a lot of photos when I studied in Paris and I enjoyed it so much that I had strong thoughts about becoming a photographer instead of a designer/illustrator. Do you feel, there is a Scandinavian (design) identity or special approach? Yes, a Swedish design identity. I think Swedish design is simple and strong. What are your inspirations, aims, dreams and what's your philosophy? One of my dreams is to live in a warm and sunny country with my family for a year, find an agent and let her send me interesting work. It would be nice to work one day and have the next day off. I work too much now, so my aim is therefor; to work less. My philosophy is to enjoy my work. And to stop when I don´t.

PIKE

Jonas Pike Dahlström
artworks on page: 113 Image, 146/147 Illustrations + projects, 176 Illustration
home country: Sweden • living/working in Stockholm, Sweden
email: pike@chello.se • url: htt://members.chello.se/pike
date of birth: 08/01/72
CV / short company history/ studies/ education: student at royal academy of fine arts (stockholm)
latest personal / commercial projects: to build the first illegal "legal graffitiwall"
Do the landscapes/dark winters/midsummer nights have an effect on your soul and design? Propably. What influence have traditional folkloristic art and pop art on your work? I don't know. What would you do if you were not a designer? I don't know. Do you feel, there is a Scandinavian (design) identity or special approach? Propably. What are your inspirations, aims, dreams and what's your philosophy? My friends inspire me and my aim is to surprise myself. My physolophy when it comes to working is, if it's boring, don't do it.

PRODUCTS OF PLAY AS

artworks on page: 028 Advertising, 050/051 Toilet signs, 055 CD cover, 128 CD cover
home country: Norway • living/working in Oslo, Norway
email: erik@playpuppy.com / marius@playpuppy.com • url:www.playpuppy.com
date of foundation: Play was born in the year 2000.
CV / short company history/ studies/ education: Play was founded by Marius Watz (alias Amoeba) and Erik Johan Worsøe Eriksen (former Hybrid Design) late 2000, to serve as a turf for both commercial and self-initiated work. As of now Play has finished projects in areas that include TV-identity, TV-spot, web design, type design, interior design, as well as regular company identities and printed stuff. About 50% of our workload comes from the music business and involves designing and art directing CD covers and promotional material.
latest personal / commercial projects: Redesigning a CD cover for Sondre Lerche for his release in the UK market, and live visuals for the outstanding norwegian jazzensemble, Wibutee.
Do the landscapes/dark winters/midsummer nights have an effect on your soul and design? Dark winters and midsummer nights, I don't know about. But the landscape is a constant inspiration and provides us with our number one tool for excercising our company policy: go play in steep mountains! What influence have traditional folkloristic art and pop art on your work? I think pop art is a heavy influence in our work, formally but even more in attitude. We tend to embrace our times and the way of our times, not work against it. What would you do if you were not a designer? We would be part of a helicopter rescue team... Do you feel, there is a Scandinavian (design) identity or special approach? In furniture, textile, architecture: yes. When it comes to graphic design it seems to be watered down by referances from all the leading design crews in USA, UK, The Netherlands, Switzerland and so on... I can see no singular Scandinavian way. Historically our profession has not stood very strong here, but the last ten years has seen an amazing upgrading of the overall quality and consiousness about what it means and it's powers... I'm very optimistic, and a little bit scared of the escalating competition. What are your inspirations, aims, dreams and what's your philosophy? Inspirations: Funky music, loud parties, good friends, tasty food, bold climbing. Aims, dreams and philosphy: Funkier music, louder parties, better friends, deliscious food, harder climbing. Get better.

PULSK RAVN / GULSTUE

artworks on page: 108 Catalogue, 141 Poster
home country: Denmark • living/working in Copenhagen, Denmark
email: mail@pulsk.dk • url: www.pulsk.dk
date of birth: 21/09/71
CV / short company history/ studies/ education: MA The Danish School of Design, Visual Communication / Graphic Design.
latest personal / commercial projects: Billboard exhibition, Copenhagen V. Contemplation Room, project in public space.
Do the landscapes/dark winters/midsummer nights have an effect on your soul and design? On my temper, yes. What influence have traditional folkloristic art and pop art on your work? Pop art has influenced both art and design history... and my work. What would you do if you were not a designer? No matter what title, my inspirations and work would be the same. Do you feel, there is a Scandinavian (design) identity or special approach? There is. What are your inspirations, aims, dreams and what's your philosophy? To keep the curiosity fresh.

SPILD AF TID APS / WASTE OF TIME INC.

artworks on page: 102 Poster I Various animations - stills
home country: Denmark • living/working in Copenhagen, Denmark
fax: +45 3535 2645
email: info@spildaftid.dk • url: www.spildaftid.dk
date of foundation: August 2000
CV / short company history/ studies/ education: Spild Af Tid was founded in august 2000 by the four illustrators/ graphic designers; Rasmus Meisler, Jakob Thorbek, Jenz Koudahl and Julie Asmussen, all of whom were educated at The Institute for Visual Communication at The Danish School of Design in Copenhagen - with detours at Konstfack College and Arts, Craft and Design in Stockholm, Academia Sztuk Pieknych in Krakow and Ravensbourne College of Design and Communication in London.
Spil af Tid is known for their harsh and satirical work expressed through drawings, motion graphic, dolls, collages and short animation films where the good and satirical story is emphasised and told with rapid cutting and a vivid sound track.
latest personal / commercial projects: KIDS (2002) Intro, breakers and animations for a new youth program. To be broadcasted this autumn. Childbooks.dk (2001-2002) Childbook website for Danish Centre of Literature Lille Skat/Little darling (2001.2003). Animated short film based on the author Jan Sonnegaards short story "Lille skat"
Do the landscapes/dark winters/midsummer nights have an effect on your soul and design? Yes, we get really depressed during winter and hysterically happy during summer.....but soon a sneaking depression comes because we realize that the summer will be over soon. What influence have traditional folkloristic art and pop art on your work? It has great influence because we do sample both from the past and from present time. What would you do if you were not a designer? Jenz and Jakob: Undercover cop, Julie: opera singer, Rasmus: butcher. Do you feel, there is a Scandinavian (design) identity or special approach? Still discussion that one.... What are your inspirations, aims, dreams and what's your philosophy? inspiration: Our neighbourhood, Music, Anti-inspired by rightwing-racists parties and: Jan Svankmajer, Egon Schiele, Hank Williams, Jaques Tati, Robert Rausenberg, Acton Friis, Elvis, se7en, Tomato, Little walter, Svend Bratch, Chris Ware, Ralp Steadman, Philip BurkeE, Saul BASS, Robert Brownjohn, Edward Weie, Helene Schierfbeck, Jean Michel Basquiat, G-love, Joni Mitchell. Aims/Dreams: creative and financial independency. Philosophy: One for all and all for one.

STYLEWAR

artworks on page: 047 Video stills
home country: Sweden • living/working in Stockholm, Sweden
fax: +46 8 662 88 95 • email: we@stylewar.com • url: www.stylewar.com
CV / short company history/ studies/ education: The company started summer 1998, today StyleWar has 7 full-time employees: one producer, two 3D-artists and four graphic designers. Current work spans from music videos, commercials and title sequences to illustrations for children's' books and print ads.
latest personal / commercial projects: Music videos: Jon Spencer Blues Explosion 'Sweet & Sour', Apex Theory 'Apossibly', Millencolin 'Kemp, The Hives 'Main Offender'. Commercials: 'MER 'Guava', Arla 'Kalla Såser'.
Do the landscapes/dark winters/midsummer nights have an effect on your soul and design? Yes, you work harder all the time, no matter what season it is. What influence have traditional folkloristic art and pop art on your work? None. What would you do if you were not a designer? Dish washer or architect. Do you feel, there is a Scandinavian (design) identity or special approach? Yes, very strict approach. What are your inspirations, aims, dreams and what's your philosophy? Top of the line, all the time!

SUBTOPIA

artworks on page: 050/05 »Costatronics« I Card, 052 Typo try-out, 053 CD cover, 066 Web Site »Mix Re«, 069 CD cover, 124 Promotional book, 125 Image, 129 CD cover, 140 Illustrations, 167 Illustration, 185 CD cover
home country: Norway • living/working in Oslo, Norway
fax: +47 22 47 76 79 • email: subtopia@subtopia.no • url: http://subtopia.no
date of foundation: Ocober 1996
CV / short company history/ studies/ education: Subtopia is a design and illustration company specializing in book, CD cover and magazine design as well as development of visual identities. Our client base is largely drawn from the cultural sector in Norway, ranging from mass market products to fine art productions. Subtopia started out in 1991 as a design collective, and has gradually grown into a tight-knit company collaborating with a rooster of freelancers. Subtopia is Marius Renberg, Stein J. Oevre, Frode Slotnes, Tora Juul and Anne Solli.
latest personal / commercial projects: Stein, commercial: "Irma Salo Jaeger", book on Norwegian artist Irma Salo. Jaeger, Press Publishing, Oslo. Stein, personal: www.neiffelink.com music website; Jerneiffel (music project); Jerseygirl and Costatronics (fonts); exploringvideo/animation, but not there yet. Marius, commercial: Redrawing and cleaning up logo for the magazine Donald Duck & Co (norways best selling comic book) in collaberation with designer Jesper Egemar. Marius, personal: Designing my new book-shelf-system and bedroom + getting back into drawing with pencils.
Do the landscapes/dark winters/midsummer nights have an effect on your soul and design? Stein: The soul; yes. The design; no, not really. Marius: Probably on our souls as Stein notes above. On the design? Hm... There is a, globaly speaking, a "watering down" of national individuality in design. National individuality is replaced with estethical-ideological differences that are global and not geographically defined. If we go back a hundred years it would be easier to find strong national impulse in the visual communication of Norway. As a young nation struggling to define its own identity. Admitedly this had more to do with illustration than "pure" type based design... What influence have traditional folkloristic art and pop art on your work? One of our trademarks have been the combination of the two. What would you do if you were not a designer? Stein: I would be a comic book artist, musician or farmer. Marius: I really don't know. The moment I realized you could make a living from making cool pictures (about 11 years old), there was no competion. Do you feel, there is a Scandinavian (design) identity or special approach? Stein: No. Maybe I'll change my mind after reading this book? Marius: There is the cliché that there is a longing for nature and the "simpler things in life" inherent in Scandinavian design. I am inclined to accept the following: At it's best, there seems to be a search for practicality in both development, production and ease-of-use at the base of much of the best scandinavian design. What are your inspirations, aims, dreams and what's your philosophy? Stein: Inspirations: Right now; the simplicity, freshness and vitality (but oh no, not the uniformity) of ELECTRO. Aims/dreams: Fulfillment of a personal vision through a similar approach to design and music, with each artform inspiring development of the other. Philosophy: Work hard/live long. Marius: Inspirations: Comix, lying on sofas, music, books, reading. Aims/dreams: Fulfillment of a personal vision through realizing ideas. Philosophy: Work hard/relax hard.

SUPERLOW

Halvor Bodin
artworks on page: 056 Dezine 3, 069 CD Covers I Catalogue Cover I Dezine 2
home country: Norway • living/working in Oslo, Norway
url: www.superlow.com
CV / short company history/ studies/ education: Virtual Garden, > May 2001, senior graphic designer/Creative Director Design, Kreativt Forum, 1999>, writer [dezine]. Superlow, 1998 >, personal art projects etc. Union Design, 1995 - March 2001, senior graphic designer, partner Megafon Design, 1994-1995, graphic designer. Subtopia, 1991-1994, graphic designer, founder Oslo International Filmfestival, 1991, co-founder Favola Film, 1989-1993, producer/

production manager/still-photographer.Freelance filmworker, 1986-1989, University of Oslo, 1984-1986, studies in political science
latest personal / commercial projects:"Black Low - The Punk Movement Was Just Hippies With Short Hair". An art exhibition by Norwegian contemporary artist Bjarne Melgaard. I designed all the elements such as a 160 pages catalogue, posters, invitation, banners and T-shirts... After an inspection of the exhibition –which was at that point not fully installed - on Friday the 3d of May the German Staatsanwaltschaft decided that opening the exhibition would be acriminal act. Reference was made to paragraph 131 from the German law and the concept of the show was condemned to be a ´Menschunwürdige Darstellung von Gewalt´, a depraved representation of violence. The mayer of the city of Herford consequently decided to forbid the opening of the exhibition andissued a written order from the police. The plan is to collaborate with Bjarne Melgaard on more exhibitions, in Kiel, Bologna and Wien. I have made a music-video for the Kiel exhibition for the Norwegian black metal band Thorns and will contribute to the visuals in the exhibition space.
Do the landscapes/dark winters/midsummer nights have an effect on your soul and design? I don´t think the nature has any effect on the designs I do. But The cold and long winter makes it easy for us to concentrate on working. What influence have traditional folkloristic art and pop art on your work? Folklore and the Norse sagas has influenced the Norwegian black metal scene and therefore the work I have done connected to Black Metal since 1994. But generally my work is not connected to folkloristic art and national identity. I am more influenced by contemporary art and music culture than pop art. What would you do if you were not a designer? Film producer as I used to be. Or working with fine arts as a full time job. Do you feel, there is a Scandinavian (design) identity or special approach? No, I do not think we can draw any relevant lines from contemporary graphic design in Scandinavia back to furniture design in the 50's and 60's. Graphic design in Scandinavia in 2002 is a part of the global design community with plenty of variations and influences from all over the World. What are your inspirations, aims, dreams and what's your philosophy? At the moment parts of the contemporary art scene inspires me. Black metal bands like Satyricon and Thorns inspires me. The ethical/political counter cultures like Attac and Adbusters inspires me. My aim is to keep moving around in the contemporary art scene and the contemporary design community and advertising industry. Try to contribute to a continious discussion about ethics, aesthetics and creative energy. Darkness is an absolute necessity to create. The only interesting place to be is on the edge between beauty and darkness.

SUPERSTAR.NO

Sigurd Kristiansen
artworks on page: 009/010 Poster, 065 Image »Wire«
home country: Norway • living/working in Oslo, Norway
email: sigurd@superstar.no • url: www.superstar.no
date of birth / date of foundation: 13/05/1975 | 01/01/2000
CV / short company history/ studies/ education: -1993: pixel art for demos and personal projects. 1993-1996: pixel art and 3d for games, worked on titles for Disney, Infogrammes, Psygnosis, Universal and Electronic Arts at Interactivision in Denmark and Funcom in Norway. 1996-1998: founded a game company and two internet-/design-agencies with friends, started doing graphic design. 1998-2000: graphic designer at Razorfish Oslo, worked on websites for norvegian corporate clients. 2000: started my one-man design company, superstar.no.
latest personal / commercial projects: Personal: identity and website for performance artist and actress Kate Pendry, deaddiana.com. Commercial: design and concept for a website for norways largest cable, internet & telecommunications provider, Telenor.
Do the landscapes/dark winters/midsummer nights have an effect on your soul and design? I get very depressed by the dark winters and try to travel to warmer countries for as long as possible in the winter. I have a lot more ideas and energy during the spring and autumn. Summer is usually too nice and sunny to get any serious work done. Much of my personal work is based on associations, so my state of mind is important for the results. What influence have traditional folkloristic art and pop art on your work? I'm not very influenced by folkloristic art, I find some pop art interesting but usually get my inspiration from russian, japanese, swiss and german schools of design. The use of colour in some scandinavian folkloristic art is interestign though. Do you feel, there is a Scandinavian (design) identity or special approach? What is often associated with scandinavian design is modernism and minimalism. I find it a bit odd that this has become the scandinavian trademark, as it is the total opposite to our folkloristic art. Many young scandinavian designers have a much more post-modern approach that I find very refreshing. What are your inspirations, aims, dreams and what's your philosophy? My inspiration comes from a lot of things, I can't really say that one there's thing that is my main source of inspiration. I find russian design traditions very interesting though. Travel and photography also helps to find new approaches and ways of thinking.

SWEDEN

artworks on page: 019 Styleguide | Label System for Jeans, 040/041 CD cover Dr. Kosmos »Reportage«, 042 Illustration, 043 Illustrations | Posters | Record sleeves, 044/045 poster Dr. Kosmos, 044/045 Illustrations for, 130 Book designs for „Pocky books"
home country: Sweden • living/working in Stockholm, Sweden
fax: +46 8 652 0033 • email: hello@swedengraphics.com • url: www.swedengraphics.com
date of foundation: 1997
CV / short company history/ studies/ education: Sweden has no official CV / company history
latest personal / commercial projects: We recently became active part-owners of the book publishing company "Pocky"

SYRUP HELSINKI

artworks on page: 013 poster, 050/051 Logo, 076 Koneisto Festival 2001 - Slogan | Poster, 077 Koneisto Festival 2002 - Mixed, 141 Web site - screens, 150 Pattern
home country: Finland • living/working in Helsinki, Finland
fax: +358 9 622 4657 • email: office@syruphelsinki.com • url: www.syruphelsinki.com
date of foundation: October 1999
CV / short company history/ studies/ education: Syrup Helsinki, started in 1999 as Soumi Design, is a visual communications studio based in the heart of Helsinki with an office in New York. In the field of visual communications Syrup Helsinki is using all mediums from web to tv and print to mobile, depending on the projects or who the studio is currently working with or for, or simply what they are eager to do at that moment.
latest personal / commercial projects: Visual identity for Koneisto festival 2002
Do the landscapes/dark winters/midsummer nights have an effect on your soul and design? Definetely, it´s all about that. Hm. Add some urban culture there, too, and there we are. Designers from the forest, playing in the dark, partying in the sun. What influence have traditional folkloristic art and pop art on your work? It depends on the project, but there are things that keep popping up. Paintings and photographs of birches and Kalevala, the mythic saga, are on our minds right now. How´ll they be seen in our work is a mystery. Anyway, influences come from various directions and sources, from the streets of NY to the beauty of building boats. What would you do if you were not a designer? We´d raise reindeers and do some fising. Do you feel, there is a Scandinavian (design) identity or special approach? Maybe, approach for purity... and humour... What are your inspirations, aims, dreams and what's your philosophy? Well, we´ve got this motto "Work or go home".

TEAM HAWAII

Anne Gustavsson / Malin Grundström
artworks on page: 092/093 Illustrations
home country: Sweden • living/working in Stockholm, Sweden
email: teamhawaii@chello.se • url: http://www.teamhawaii.info
date of birth / date of foundation: 1970/74 | 11/2001
CV / short company history/ studies/ education: Konstskolan | Sthlm, Basis, Nyckelviksskolan, Forsbergs and finally Beckmans school of design. We met at Beckmans, class of 2001. We did our graduation project togheter, Schweiz oder? A fake documentary which questioned the existence of Switzerland.
latest personal / commercial projects: A recent project is the graphic concept for Tom Levin who releases his debut album.
Do the landscapes/dark winters/midsummer nights have an effect on your soul and design? We don´t know really since Stockholm is the only place we have lived in. What influence have traditional folkloristic art and pop art on your work? It´s hard to say if it affects our work, niehter is a big source ofinspiration. What would you do if you were not a designer? Anne would be a hairdresser and Malin would be a drummer. Do you feel, there is a Scandinavian (design) identity or special approach? Yes, Scandinavian design is often thought of as minimalistic, a clichée that still lives. We don´t go for that approach, viva la maximalismus! What are your inspirations, aims, dreams and what's your philosophy? Our inspiration is the man in the street. We don´t dream - we live. Our philosophy is to think big and stay true to the chicks we are.

THE LEGALIZER

Robotniks (workers): Leo Scherfig, Ib Kjeldsmark, Jakob Olrik (Boss)
artworks on page: 088-091 Scetch book - images
home country: Denmark • living/working in Copenhagen, Denmark
fax: +45 3333 0264 • email: info@legalizer.dk • url: www.legalizer.dk
date of birth / date of foundation: Legalizer founded 1/1-2001. Robotniks born around 1970.
CV / short company history/ studies/ education: Jakob Olrik is a project-guy. He has been working the last ten years with theater, working-unions, music, ecology, NGO's and stuff like that. Now he is our boss. Ib Kjeldsmark graduated from Denmarks Design School in '97, and has been working maily as an illustrator since. With the Legalizer, he has turned out to be a great graphic designer, and also a great guy in association with flash-people, doing computer-games on the internet. Leo Scherfig, was making comics for small magazines before Design School, graduated in '96. Founded e-Types together with four other graphic designers, and left the company in '99 because of boredom, jazz and grumpy people. The Legalizer started as 3 guys with a desire for working with stuff that matters. Now we are 12, project-people, web-people and graphic-people.
latest personal / commercial projects: We do very varied stuff, both when it comes to topics and style. We won 1st prize at the Kemi Comics Festival in Finland, which is quite underground; and yesterday we finished a presentation of a series of stamps for the royal danish mail, which is kind of high profile. We like to do skateboard-design and book-covers, but most of all we are magazine-people. Right now we are developing on a magazine-project, called BlackBox.
Do the landscapes/dark winters/midsummer nights have an effect on your soul and design? Soul, yes. Design, it's hard to tell. Maybe what effects our soul the most could be a political climate? Please recognize that we have in Denmark a close-to-fascist regime, with no regard towards humanity, sharing, nature nor love. All that matters is hate and money. So sometimes we are very hateful, and sometimes we try to fight the evil powers with love. What influence have traditional folkloristic art and pop art on your work? None. Or; how can we tell? We are all interested in old school art, in ethnic music (but mainly asian-african), and so on. Maybe our ancestors left a gene for appreciation of special danish table-dancing, but it hasn't really shown until now. Mostly, what inspires us is energy, some dynamic music. People. And for my own part I must say that what keeps me going very energetically on is how spoilt we are in northern Europe. We have everything, so if we do not take advantage of that, and use it for something important or good, we are not worthy! Maybe that is kind of folkloristic? What would you do if you were not a designer? Ib would rock full-time in his band Rutcave, and Leo would be their promotor/manager/driver. Jakob would be the roadie in order to try to pick up girls. Do you feel, there is a Scandinavian (design) identity or special approach? Yes, one that we hate. Because of all the old furniture-guys, the younger generation thinks that cleanlyness is essential, if you want to work with design in Scandinavia. So everybody likes Wallpaper-kind-of-stuff. We don't. Still, there are lots of people who rock hard. What are your inspirations, aims, dreams and what's your philosophy? We want to rock the world of graphic bollocks, have a nice day; brain-cracking love-bullets, all fun and no play; non-stop action design.

THOMAS BRODAHL / XTRAPOP

artworks on page: 138 Illustrations
home country: Norway • living/working in London, England
email: x@xtrapop.com • url: www.xtrapop.com / www.surfstation.lu
date of birth / date of foundation: 19/10/1977 | 25/03/01
CV / short company history/ studies/ education: Born in Norway. Moved to Luxembourg when I was 10. Went to the University of Virginia in 1996. Took a 3 hr HTML course. Dropped out of school. Returned to Luxembourg to become a full-time webdesigner. Worked a couple of years. Started Surfstation.lu. Quit my job, and stated XTRAPOP. Moved to London in the fall of 2001. Currently freelancing.
latest personal / commercial projects: Surfstation.lu / Freelance work for Nike, L'Oreal, Coca Cola, MTV.
Do the landscapes/dark winters/midsummer nights have an effect on your soul and design? Well I moved away when I was quite young, well before I discovered my creative side. I guess that some of my Norwegian roots still linger with me though, and that could explain why i'm so partial to bright colors and my aversion to black.... its the memory of those dark months! What influence have traditional folkloristic art and pop art on your work? I'm a huge fan of Scandinavian design, ranging from product design all the way to the up-and-coming film-makers. I don;t think that they are particularly influential in my design style, but they certainly are part of my sense of aesthetics. What would you do if you were not a designer? I have no clue. Its a good thing I figured out something I was good at. Do you feel, there is a Scandinavian (design) identity or special approach? I think that because of the strict climate and the protestant values, scandinavians are very focused on functionality, and out of that we have managed to create a new aesthetic. If you go to southern europe and look at catholic architecture and art, it is the complete opposite. What are your inspirations, aims, dreams and what's your philosophy? Inspirations are all around. I'm blessed to be working with so many of my favorite designers, and I learn from them all the time. My aim is to keep doing what I love and at some point reach the level that I want to be at. It is so great to be able to make a living off of your hobby, so I am just gonna consider myself fortunate as long as I can keep that up.

THORMAR MELSTED

artworks on page: 039 Image
home country: Iceland • living/working in Seltjarnarnes, Iceland
email: thormar@weirdhabits.is • url: www.weirdhabits.is
date of birth: 22/03/79
CV / short company history/ studies/ education: worked at Deluxe designhouse im at the Universty of Iceland Designappartment, worked just for someone or just me
latest personal / commercial projects: Cover for Singapore sling, a show at the art museum of Reykjavik.
Do the landscapes/dark winters/midsummer nights have an effect on your soul and design? Wake up late / work hard / drink mudch / Meet people /something very good comes out of that. Just try it. The landscape has something to say but I cant say what. It is just something that I got when I was born as an Icelandic. What influence have traditional folkloristic art and pop art on your work? Maybe something but I dont know were it comes from and I hope that I never will find out. But it is good to discover other's peoples work and find out whot kind of people they are or they were, everything counts. What would you do if you were not a designer? Record shop owner or a sheff. Do you feel, there is a Scandinavian (design) identity or special approach? Dont think so. Maybe... What are your inspirations, aims, dreams and what's your philosophy? My friends, everyday people, everything around me, that I will always find something new and people will never stop making music and something wiil always surprisse me. Surprise anyone anytime anywere.

TORSTEN HØGH RASMUSSEN / GULSTUE

artworks on page: 184 Movie stills/ production design for an animated movie
home country: Denmark • living/working in Copenhagen, Denmark
email: torsten@gulstue.com
date of birth / date of foundation: 08.04.72 | 01.01.01
CV / short company history/ studies/ education: Masters degree from the Danish Designschool 2000. Work as productiondesigner on the shortfilm "Provins". Different jobs including illustration, layout, design and postproduction for films, fonts, posters and such.
latest personal / commercial projects: Productiondesign for a film made at the Danish Film School / Visuel identity for Copenhagen Philharmonic Orchestra
Do the landscapes/dark winters/midsummer nights have an effect on your Soul and design? The clear, bright light of the afternoons at wintertime tend to appear in my work. Here and there. What influence have traditional folkloristic art and pop art on your work? I´m influenced by the old danish typographers. But more by the russian, though. What would you do if you were not a designer? I´d like to be a beekeeper on Samsø... Do you feel, there is a Scandinavian (design) identity or special approach? Absolutely, straight lines and no colors.

TRIPTYKON

Masoud Alavi / Peter Rössell
artworks on page: 057 Logo - video still | Christmas card
home country: Denmark • living/working in Copenhagen, Denmark
fax: +45 3332 8886 • email: mail@triptykon.com • url: www.triptykon.com
date of foundation: 1997

VÅR

artworks on page: 038 Book cover, 094/095 Illustrations, 139 Illustrations, 167 Illustration, 202 Wallpaper, 203 Magazine illustrations | Wallpaper, 207 Wallpaper, 212-217 Wallpapers
home country: Sweden • living/working in Stockholm, Sweden
fax: +46 8 6120600 • email: grandin@ot.se / bjorn@ot.se • url: www.woo.se
date of foundation: 1996
CV / short company history/ studies/ education: 'Vår' is the Swedish word meaning both 'Spring' and 'Ours', it is also the name of Stockholm-based illustration design team Karl Grandin and Björn Kärvestedt. Their work has been exhibited at various galleries in Sweden, and at Gallery Speak FOR and the Parco Logos in Tokyo. Vår's work can also be found on t-shirts, book covers, album covers and magazines. Recent projects include Mikrofonkåt (a book about Swedish hip hop), cover art for Penguin Books, and illustrations for magazines like Commons & Sense, Tokion, Harper's Bazaar, Vogues Hommes International and Wallpaper. Check our work at www.woo.se
What influence have traditional folkloristic art and pop art on your work? Of course things like travelling, experiencing new things, stuff like that inspire us. I guess a lot of Scandinavian and Swedish things also have a great influence on us but it's harder to point out exactly what goes into our work. What would you do if you were not a designer? Chill. Fish. Do you feel, there is a Scandinavian (design) identity or special approach? Maybe all countries, societies, or whatever, develop some kind of conformity within the group. But I think young Swedish designers today have a great variety of influences, rather than looking back on some kind of 'Scandinavian design tradition' people look abroad for inspiration. Today there are people from all over the world living in Scandinavia (as well as the rest of the world) and things are changing all the time so I don't think it's very interesting to think too much about 'national identity' and shit like that. What are your inspirations, aims, dreams and what's your philosophy? We try to change and develop all the time, do new things in new ways. And we should try to get better at doing that.

VILUNKI 3000 / SPEED GRAPHICS

artworks on page: 135 Record sleeve
home country: Finland • living/working in Helsinki, Finland
email: vilunki3000@editstation.fi
Look out for the Op:l Bastards!

VIRTUAL GARDEN

see Superlow
artworks on page: 026/027 identity, 053 Book scetches, 056 Identity

ZORGLOB

Oscar Bjarnason
artworks on page: 025, 050/051, 128/129 Images/Illustrations
home country: Iceland • living/working in Reykjavik, Iceland
email: oscar@zorglob.com • url: http://zorglob.com
date of birth / date of foundation: July 30st, 1976
CV / short company history/ studies/ education: Bought my first computer 1997 but started looking into design in 1998. Worked for some small printshops for 2 years before applying at an ad-agency here in iceland as a print designer. Worked there for about a year before I was bought over to my current job here at Fiskar (http://fiskar.is). Here I've gained experience in web designing as well as motion design on top of the print experience I had before.
latest personal / commercial projects: Latest commercial project I did for the web that i'm happy with, was http://spessi.com ..clean and simple site made in 4 working days for a respected photographer here in iceland. Latest personal project would have to be http://zorglob.com. It's always in the making and will never be 100% finnished due to my constant ambition to do something new, something I've not done before.
Do the landscapes/dark winters/midsummer nights have an effect on your soul and design? Yeah definitely ...when the summer sneaks up on us I tend to get all "loveble" in my designs ...and when the winter comes I tend to get a bit darker so seasons and landscape do definitely have a huge inpact on my soul as a designer. What influence have traditional folkloristic art and pop art on your work? I really don't know for sure ...I bet they have some influence but I don't know what. What would you do if you were not a designer? A musician ..love music ..played keyboards long before I got my firscomputer. Do you feel, there is a Scandinavian (design) identity or special approach? Yeah I think so ...but these days you can't be shoure whitch design is from where due to the huge amount of inspirations on the web and through books ..everyone is doing all sorts of designs so it's pretty hard to tell where it's from. What are your inspirations, aims, dreams and what's your philosophy? My inspirations are found all over ...daily life, outdoors, books, web, tv, movies, people, words and you name it. My aims are to live life to the fullest and do better designs. I'm living a part of my dream now ...making a living doing the thing that I love, design. In my future dreams there is my own design studio just to mention one thing. My philosophy is: everything is possible if you set your mind to it.

Page 002 - Foreword by Goddur »North by North - Remix«
Page 040 - Interview with Sweden
Page 062 - Feature by Kaliber10000 »Scandinavian Web Design«
Page 096 - Feature by Thomas Hilland »The Shocking Truth«
Page 040 - Interview with EkhornForss/Non-Format

Thanks to all contributors.
For more information about the artists/artworks: please look at the artists websites or contact them directly.

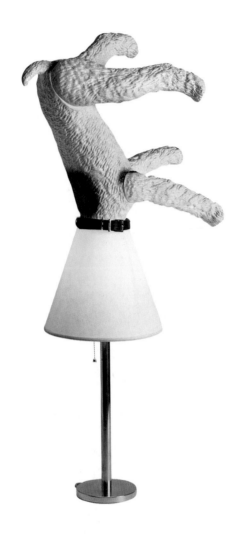

NORTH BY NORTH

Edited by Robert Klanten, Hendrik Hellige and Måns Nyman.
Layout and executive management by Hendrik Hellige. Contacts, executive management and logistics Sweden by Måns Nyman. Contacts Iceland supported by Goddur.
Proof-reading: Sonja Commentz/Simpeltext. Technical supervision: Janine Milstrey. Technical assistance: Katja Haub.

ISBN 3-931126-91-9 – Die Deutsche Bibliothek-CIP Einheitsaufnahme: Ein Titeldatensatz für diese Publikation ist bei der Deutschen Bibliothek erhältlich.

Printed by Medialis Offset, Berlin. Made in Europe.